Basic Home
Networking

Roderico DeLeon
Ted Coombs

THOMSON

DELMAR LEARNING

Australia • Canada • Mexico • Singapore • Spain • United Kingdom • United States

THOMSON
DELMAR LEARNING

Basic Home Networking
Roderico DeLeon and Ted Coombs

Business Unit Director:
Alar Elken

Executive Editor:
Sandy Clark

Senior Acquisitions Editor:
Gregory L. Clayton

Development:
Jennifer Luck

Executive Marketing Manager:
Maura Theriault

Channel Manager:
Fair Huntoon

Marketing Coordinator:
Karen Smith

Executive Production Manager:
Mary Ellen Black

Production Manager:
Larry Main

Production Editor:
Stacy Masucci

Art/Design Coordinator:
David Arsenault

Library of Congress Cataloging-in-Publication Data:

ISBN: 0-7668-6180-5

This book is dedicated to all who have found and
all who will find love over a network.

Contents

Acknowledgments		*ix*
Chapter 1	**Introduction to Home Networking**	**1**
	Networking Background	2
	Networks in the Home	4
	What it Takes	5
	Using Your Network	6
Chapter 2	**Choosing the Right Type of Home Network**	**9**
	Wireless Networks	11
	HomeRF	12
	Wi–Fi	14
	Infrared	17
	Bluetooth	18
	Wired Networks	20
	Home Phone Lines	20
	Power Lines	23
	Ethernet	24
	USB and Firewire	27
Chapter 3	**Setting up the Hardware**	**31**
	Cables and Wires	32
	Network Interface Cards	39
	Hubs	46
	Phone-Line Connections	50
	Setting up Wireless LANS	53

Chapter 4	**Setting up a Home Network**	**57**
	Planning the Network Layout	59
	What You Will Need	63
	Installing the Cable	69
	Phoneline and Powerline Networks	75
	Fiber Network Planning	81
	Wireless Networks	83

Chapter 5	**Configuring Software**	**87**
	Basic Information	88
	Static vs. Dynamic IP Addresses	88
	Your Network IP Address	89
	The Mechanics of an IP Address	91
	Default Gateways	94
	Your IP Address and You	95
	Network Setup in Windows 95, 98, Me, and 2000	100
	Installing Network Components	102
	Setting up a Wireless Network Card	103
	Domain Names	104

Chapter 6	**Network Sharing**	**109**
	Getting Started	110
	Shared Printers	110
	Attaching the Printer to the Computer	111
	Configuring Printer Sharing	111
	Sharing Folders and Files	120
	File Sharing on the Macintosh	129
	Network Neighborhood	131
	Mapping a Network Drive	132
	Computer Sharing	133
	Remote Desktop Connection	137

Chapter 7	**Sharing the Internet**	**145**
	Routers	146
	DHCP Servers	151
	Proxy Servers and Firewalls	155
	ICS (Internet Connection Sharing)	158

Chapter 8   **Managing Your Home Network**   **163**
              Training   164
              Protecting Your Network   165
              Threats to Security   166
              Preventing Losses   170

Chapter 9   **Troubleshooting the Network**   **177**
              Is it Plugged In?   178
              Additional Hardware Issues   180
              Tools for Hardware Troubleshooting   180
              Configuration Troubles   181
              Testing the Connection   185
              Tracing the Connection Path   187
              Assorted Network Problems   189
              When All Else Fails   191

Chapter 10   **Home of the Future**   **195**
              Universal Plug and Play   196
              Home Automation   197
              Video   200
              Home Games Consoles   201
              Wireless Roaming   202
              The Car   202
              Out There   203
              Pen Tablets: Notebooks of the Future   205

Appendix   **209**

Where to Go for More Information   **213**

Glossary   **215**

Index   **231**

Acknowledgments

We would like to acknowledge everyone who helped us with the creation of this book. In particular, we'd like to thank Greg Clayton and Jennifer Luck, and a special thanks to our family for supporting us while writing this book—literally.

Introduction to Home Networking 1

Language and communication are often thought to be some of the essential attributes of being human. From the early days of jungle drums and smoke signals, it has been a human endeavor to communicate over long distances. The modern communications network had its origins in 1793, with the development of the French Optical Telegraph Network. This network relied on a series of cross arms and pulleys to display a message that could be read from a distance by someone watching through a telescope.

Network technology has advanced a great deal in the last 200 years. From the French Optical Telegraph Network sprang the telegraph, the telephone, and eventually computer networks.

Networks have changed the way machines and people communicate, not only for business purposes but for entertainment as well. Originally, computers merely used networks for the purpose of sharing data and printers. Wiring computers together in a network created a cost savings by allowing several computers to share the same printer and the same hard drive. Now, they are used to enable communication over the Internet, control home appliances, play multiuser games, and, of course, share printers, hard drives, and other devices.

Networking Background

Computer networks existed in the early days of commercial computers—in the 1950s. Computers then were large mainframe computers whose only access was via a remote *dumb terminal*. These dumb terminals were essentially keyboards, a monitor, and a primitive modem. They were wired to the mainframe computer in much the same way as computers are wired today using networks. This was a very efficient and cost-effective way to allow access to a mainframe computer from many places, without the necessity of putting a computer at every location. These wired "networks" also allowed the sharing of expensive, high-speed line printers.

There were, and still are, upsides to this centralized way of computing. The invention of the desktop computer in the late 1970s and early 1980s created a new demand for decentralized data. Personal computers (PCs) allowed individual company departments, and sometimes even individual companies, to own and have immediate access to their data. Programmers were able to write customized programs to enter and access data without having to wait for year-long waiting lists for mainframe programmers to write applications.

It was not very long after the invention of the PC that people began wanting some of the advantages of the terminal and mainframe. Special cards were invented that allowed PCs to also act like dumb terminals, eliminating the need for both a PC and a terminal on someone's desk. Eventually, it was also possible to move data from the mainframe to the PC for local processing by applications running on the desktop.

At about this same time, local area networks were invented that allowed PCs to communicate with one another—sharing hard drives and printers. The networks were expensive and the cable was as big around as your thumb. The immediate cost savings from not having to buy everyone their own printer created an immediate payback for installing networks. Even though the early networks had sophisticated file and application sharing, very few programs were written to take advantage of these capabilities, and even fewer computer users knew how to use their network to its fullest potential.

Even with the challenges faced by network users, cable quickly began winding its way through every corporate office. This created the next challenge—how to hook the networks together so that users could communicate between networks. The challenge here was that these often included different computer types and different network brands. Apple computers used an AppleTalk network and PCs could choose from a number of different and nonstandard network types, the two most popular being Novell and IBM.

The answer to this was ethernet and TCP/IP—the hardware and software (respectively) that brought a commonality to the many network brands. Networks could now communicate with other networks.

Ethernet was invented by Robert Metcalfe at the Xerox Palo Alto Research Center. He was attempting to build a network for Xerox computers to take advantage of another technology they were building—the first laser printer. In 1979, when Metcalfe left Xerox, he convinced Xerox, Intel, and Digital Equipment to use ethernet hardware as the standard for network communications.

TCP/IP, a suite of network communications protocols, is software that enables computer-to-computer communications. It was created in the early

1970s as part of a Department of Defense (DoD) project to connect various DoD research sites. This network project, originally called ARPANet (Advanced Research Project Agency Network), grew from the connection of a few college campuses to a worldwide network by the early 1970s.

The hardware and software developed for the ARPANet formed the foundation of today's Internet as well as most Local Area Networks (LANs). The network you are now considering for your home uses this technology, which has been developed over the last 40 years.

Networks in the Home

According to a study by the U.S. Department of Education, the number of homes in America with multiple PCs will reach 31 million in 2002. The reasons for this sharp increase in homes sporting more than one computer include the plummeting price of home computers, always-on dedicated Internet connections, and the increased dependence on computers for communication.

The benefits and challenges of network installation is the same for homes as for businesses. Home networking allows a home to receive the benefits of

- Shared Internet access
- Network sharing
- File sharing
- Application sharing
- Network-based gaming

In this book, we offer real-world examples of how home networks can simplify life in the home, reduce equipment costs, and safeguard your computer network by providing easy backup and network-based virus protection.

What it Takes

Your first task in preparing for a home network is to decide which type of network you want to purchase. There are two main varieties—the type that require wires and a newer type of network that allows you to connect computers without wires, operating in much the same manner as a cordless phone.

Chapter 2 walks you through the various types of networks, and helps you decide which network type is best for you. There is a myriad of types to choose from, as Figure 1.1 shows. Brands and capabilities change over time but the fundamentals will remain the same, allowing you to evaluate new technologies as they emerge.

Figure 1.1 *Select a network based on its capabilities, not the color of the box.*

Once you have decided on a network type, the next step is installation. Chapter 3 discusses the hardware you will need and Chapter 4 walks you through the physical installation of both wired and wireless networks. Running network cable is a bit of a chore and wireless networks are subject to noise and interference, but both network types have their distinct advantages. Wireless networks are definitely easier to install than wired networks.

The procedure for configuring your operating system to use the network and installing the software drivers for the network card is pretty much the same for both types of networks. Installing the network card drivers is almost automatic when you turn on the power to your computer. Configuring the network settings is a little trickier, but will take less than 10 minutes of your time. After that, your network will be up and running. Chapter 5 will cover these software-configuration tasks.

Using your Network

Once your network is up and running you will want to know how to make the best use of it. The network will allow you to share hard drives and printers, and use network-ready software. Until recently, the number one reason to create networks was to share information and printers. With the popularity of the Internet, the reason has shifted to give Internet access to more than one computer through a single Internet connection. Chapters 6 and 7 will help you make the most of your network by teaching you the fundamentals of using your network and sharing an Internet connection between all of the computers on your network.

As with just about anything else, caring for your network properly will help it provide efficient, trouble-free operation and last longer. Chapter 8 will bring you up to speed on the care and feeding of your home network (including backup). Computers break. This is a simple, unavoidable fact. How serious the consequences are to you depends on two things—how important the information stored on the computer is to you and the care you have taken to ensure that the damage from even a catastrophic failure of your computer is minimized through proper backup. Networks can make backing up your computers simpler.

If you run into difficulty, or you think your network is not operating properly, the tools and tips described in Chapter 9 will help you identify and even correct the problems in most cases. Of course, as with anything else, things break. If you determine that your network equipment is failing, you will want to contact either the store from which you purchased it or the manufacturer for assistance or return information.

Chapter 10 talks about some of the technologies on the market now and some that are in the works. There is no doubt that our homes, our cars, and our lives will be tied together by technology.

Summary

Installing a home network is not difficult. This book will give you the fundamentals to not only make the installation go more smoothly, but also give you a deeper understanding of what you are doing as you do it. This information will provide a good foundation for deciding on future technologies to incorporate into your network as you move toward having the home of the future. The futuristic home is already here, and there is much more on the horizon.

The adventure begins with choosing the type of network you will install. If you have already chosen or purchased network equipment, you should read Chapter 2 anyway. You may find out more about your network—its capabilities and limitations. You will also learn how this equipment will or will not interoperate with other networks.

One friendly warning: be patient. Your patience is required for a number of reasons. First, there is a shock hazard when working with electrical devices. Second, you may be running cable or installing wireless equipment in high places. Lastly, network software operates in such a way that problems are not always apparent. Careful and methodical troubleshooting will usually lead to a quick resolution.

Choosing the Right Type of Home Network 2

There are several types of networking hardware. This chapter introduces the different ways to build a home network. You may select one of the wireless options—either infrared or radio-based. You will also learn about how easy it is to set up a simple phoneline network and to use ethernet when speed and power are important.

Every household is different and every network is different. It is important to choose the correct network for your home. You should consider the following:

- Bandwidth requirements
- Cost
- Ease of installation
- Ease of use

The first two items in the list, bandwidth requirements and cost, will probably affect your choice of a network more than how easy it is to install and use. The network you choose, once it is installed and running, is just as easy to use as most others.

Bandwidth, measured in bits per second, is the amount of digital information that can be sent from one computer to another in a given amount of time. It is similar to measuring the amount of water that can flow through a hose in gallons per minute—the bigger the hose, the more water that can flow. Networks are very similar. It is not the *size* of the wire that affects how much data can flow, but factors affecting bandwidth are many (including the *type* of wire).

Each network technology has its own unique set of limits on bandwidth. Some limits are based on the type of wire that is used. In wireless networks, they are based on how much data can be sent across a radio signal. Ultimately, bandwidth affects computer performance when performing tasks such as loading a Web page across the network, moving files from one computer to another, or sending files to a printer.

This chapter will help you better understand how each type of network performs, the bandwidth available to you, and a little about the cost of each type of network. We will give you some reasons for purchasing a certain type of network, and some reasons you might want to consider another type of network.

When choosing a network, or any computer equipment, it is always wise to choose a company that has a good reputation for quality equipment—and most importantly, accessible and sound technical support.

To get started, you should know that there are six basic varieties of home networks based on how each network transmits information from one computer to another:

- Wireless
- Phoneline
- Powerline
- Ethernet
- USB
- Firewire

Wireless Networks

Wireless networks are relatively new in the world of computer networking. Sending data over the airwaves, however, dates back to 1905 when telegraph signals sent the first message (S.O.S) via radio waves. During World War II, encrypted data was sent over radio waves enabling complex battle plans to be sent over enemy lines. It was around 25 years after the end of the World War II that the first wireless LAN was conceived. In 1971, ALOHANET allowed seven computers on four of the Hawaiian Islands to communicate in a star pattern with its primary hub at the University of Hawaii on Oahu.

The type of network formed in Hawaii was known as a packet radio network, sending "packets" of information across radio waves. In 1978, packet radio was first introduced to the world of amateur radio. Ham radio operators began creating a worldwide network of computers interconnected via packet radio.

The Home Networking Standards

Today there are several competing types of wireless home networks. We will discuss some of each type's features, advantages, and disadvantages. It appears that the 802.11 standard, the last item in the following list, will emerge to remain the industry standard for wireless networking.

- HomeRF
- Bluetooth
- Infrared
- Wi-Fi or 802.11 (including AirPort for Macs)

As with any type of network, wireless networks have their advantages and disadvantages. In the following sections, we discuss both types of networks to find out which might be the right wireless solution for your home.

HomeRF

Home Radio Frequency (HomeRF) is an alliance of network equipment manufacturers that has recently developed a wireless network standard called Share Wireless Access Protocol (SWAP). It is a standard for a very low-power radio frequency-based network. HomeRF currently offers 1.6 Mbps bandwidth, although the FCC has approved a new technology that will increase the speed of HomeRF to 10 Mbps. New equipment that supports this speed is scheduled to be on the market soon.

Companies like Intel and Proxim are already supplying full HomeRF systems. Both of these companies supply good equipment and back them up with technical support.

When retrieving streaming media (music and video broadcasts) from the Internet, HomeRF has the advantage over other wireless network types. HomeRF has built-in support for multimedia applications. Along with music and video, HomeRF is also designed to work well with your telephone system, allowing you to transmit high-quality voice through the network.

Companies such as SimpleDevices (*http://www.simpledevices.com*) are developing products that will connect to your network, such as the SimpleFi home stereo, which uses the Internet as the source of the stereo broadcast. You can also listen to MP3s (the latest in digital music), Internet radio programs, or almost any other media type for which you would normally use your computer to listen. This company offers other devices such as a networked writing pad and a networked clock.

Why Choose HomeRF?

Consider choosing a HomeRF network if you are networking two or three PCs in your home, and if the people using them are not all going to download multimedia files from the Internet simultaneously. HomeRF, as we mention in more detail in Chapter 3, is considered a Personal Area Network (PAN), and is not as ready for heavy use as a LAN. However, here are some advantages to consider:

- Inexpensive
- Easy to install
- No cables or wires
- Connects up to 127 devices per network
- Reliable and standards-based
- Power-saving modes
- Higher multimedia and voice support than competing wireless networks

Why Not Choose HomeRF?

When your network requirements are heavy, such as running a home office while kids are using their computers in other rooms, and dad is in the kitchen downloading recipes, HomeRF is not optimal. This kind of use can bring even industrial-strength networks to their knees. All of the bandwidth is consumed on the network, and all of the computers using the network will notice a significant decrease in network speed or throughput. The following are some other things to consider when thinking about HomeRF:

- Limited range (about 75 to 125 feet inside) between devices and hub
- Physical obstructions (such as walls and other large things normally found in homes) can interfere with or completely block communications between devices on the network

- Not as widely adopted as other wireless standard such as Wi-Fi, discussed in the next section
- Difficult to interconnect with existing wired networks (Wireless networks are some times additions to existing wired networks.)

Wi-Fi

Wi-Fi is short for Wireless Fidelity and has another even more cumbersome name: IEEE 802.11b HR. This network type uses a networking standard known as wireless ethernet, considered one of its major advantages over Home-RF. Wi-Fi-based networks will operate with existing ethernet networks.

Wi-Fi is not a brand of network, but rather an industry standard to which many manufacturers can manufacture products. This standard employs a technique for delivering quality data signals called DSSS (Direct Sequence Spread Spectrum), which allows a data rate of up to 11 Mbps. It is *up to* 11 Mbps because Wi-Fi networks have the ability to slow down the data rate whenever interference begins to cause a loss of signal quality. The devices can drop back to 5.5 Mbps, 2 Mbps, or even to 1 Mbps if the signal is disrupted or the quality of data transfer is less than optimal. This speed adjustment keeps the network stable and very reliable.

Because Wi-Fi-compliant networks do not have the frequency-hopping capability of HomeRF, they rely on brute force in terms of power to deliver a high-quality signal. This idea is similar to sound systems of the past that were once known as Hi-Fi (which stood for High Fidelity) because of the improved sound quality they were able to deliver over earlier radios.

Wi-Fi has been used largely by the business community because of its ability to interoperate with existing ethernet networks. Very recently, home-network products have become available on the market.

Large companies are already using Wi-Fi technology, giving their employees the ability to connect to this type of network by using PC cards or other devices. These make connecting to Wi-Fi networks at home simple. In addition to using Wi-Fi technology at home and at work, some companies are already offering Wi-Fi wireless Internet access in hotels, airports, and Internet cafes. Even Starbucks is planning to launch this service in their coffee shops.

Because ethernet has never been the perfect network standard for streaming media, this same weakness is found in its wireless versions as well. This challenge has been met by ShareWave (*http://www.sharewave.com*), a company that has developed an enhancement for the 802.11b version of Wi-Fi. They call it Whitecap and base it on the 802.11e standard. Whitecap uses a network standard called QoS (Quality of Service). This enables better scheduling of network resources and thus better traffic control on your home network.

Wireless connections claim distance ratings from testing in a perfect world. For example, the 300 feet claimed by Wi-Fi can be reached if you happen to be in the same very large room or the same open space as the device to which you are trying to connect. Once you start adding walls, pets, furniture, and interference, you are probably looking at closer to a 150 foot working range.

A newer version, designated 802.11a, is broadcast at 5 GHz and allows data transfer rates up to 54 Mbps. The versioning of these products can be confusing. The newer standard ends in the letter "a" while the older standard ends with the letter "b". Clearly, the increased bandwidth of 802.11a does not come without a price. The 300+ foot ranges of 802.11b devices have five times the 60 foot range of 802.11a. This does not limit your network to only 60 feet—you simply need to install more wireless access points (transceivers) to allow for coverage over a greater distance. Sixty feet may be sufficient coverage, however, for the areas of your home where you would like network coverage.

Note: The two 802.11 standards will not always interoperate. When mixing technologies it is important to select equipment that supports both 802.11a and 802.11b standards.

When considering which of the 802.11 standards to use, you must weigh cost versus performance. The older version, 802.11b, is cheaper and provides greater coverage, potentially requiring fewer access points. The speed of 802.11b is comparable to the speed of most wired home networks: 10 Mbps. The downside to 802.11b is that it operates at 2.4 GHz, a frequency now in use by newer-model cordless telephones and most microwave ovens. These two devices could potentially interfere with one another. Operating a network at 5

GHz (as you would with the 802.11a version) currently puts a device outside the range of most other home products.

When choosing a wireless solution, 802.11 seems to be a sensible answer. This standard has gained wide support worldwide and is being developed further. For example, engineering is taking place that will allow computers equipped with wireless network cards to roam using the digital cellular telephone system.

Wi-Fi for the Mac

Wi-Fi is not just for the Windows PC. AirPort, a collaboration between Apple Computer and Lucent Technologies, lets you network your iBook, iMac, PowerBook G4, Power Mac G4 Cube, or Power Mac G4 computer without wires (*http://www.apple.com/airport/*). These Apple computers are currently the only ones in the Mac line that are compatible with the AirPort network. AirPort currently supports only the 802.11b standard.

 Note: The AirPort software version 2.0 includes the technology necessary to work with many DSL and cable modems for Internet access.

To use AirPort you have to install the AirPort card and have an AirPort base station or a computer that is acting as a base station. The AirPort base station also comes with a built-in 56k modem so you simply plug the modem into a phone line with a standard telephone cable. You are ready for Internet access, but with one notable exception—AirPort is not currently compatible with America Online.

Versions of 802.11a products are also available for the Macintosh computer. Proxim makes 802.11 products for both the Windows and Macintosh computers (*http://www.proxim.com*). This line of equipment supports both 802.11a and 802.11b in their Harmony line of products.

Why Choose Wi-Fi?
- Fast data transmission (11 Mbps and 54 Mbps)
- Reliability using speed adjustment
- Mobility – a plus with any wireless technology
- No cables or wires

- It has a good range—between 250 and 300 feet for 802.11b devices
- Compatible and easy to integrate with existing wired ethernet network
- Easy to integrate with other Wi-Fi networks
- Heavily supported by the computer industry

Why Not Choose Wi-Fi?

- Tends to be more expensive than other wireless network options
- Requires an access point (base)
- Physical obstructions (such as walls) can interfere with communications between devices
- Not always easy to set up
- Speed can fluctuate significantly due to interference with household devices like phones and microwaves

Infrared

Infrared design is based on technology that is similar to the remote controls for TVs, stereos, and VCRs. Information is sent using a beam of light not visible to the human eye. We include this discussion of infrared networking, not to suggest it as a means to permanently network two or more computers, but because infrared networking has become a common way to intermittently connect peripheral devices such as printers, handheld computers, and even data watches and watch cameras.

There are serious restrictions to infrared networking that have kept it from competing with other wireless network technologies such as HomeRF or Wi-Fi for serious intercomputer communications.

- **Speed** – 9,600 to 115,200 bits per second is slow compared to the one to two million bits per second of even the slowest radio network.
- **Line of Site** – Because Infrared is a beam of light, the light path must be fairly unobstructed. We say *fairly unobstructed* because infrared light has some ability to bend around objects because of its very long wavelength.

Infrared (IR) networks may not zip along like other networks, but they shine when it comes to inexpensive, mobile, or intermittent connections. You can walk up to your PC with your palmtop and transfer small files or calendar data. You can point your camera watch at a PC and download photos. You can even print to a printer on the other side of the room without bulky printer cables.

Devices equipped with IR can be quickly linked into your network. Some of the newer IR network protocols even allow network data connections to the Internet. This technology should not be considered as an alternative to other network types, but as a great addition to any home network. Chances are good that in the future more and more home appliances will be equipped with IR data ports.

Why Choose IR?

- Inexpensive
- Reliable
- No cables or wires
- Most notebooks and handheld computers come with this technology
- Minimal interference

Why Not Choose IR?

- Limited range
- Direct line of sight—Nothing can stand between the communicating devices to block the signal

Bluetooth

Bluetooth technology is a short-range (up to 33 feet) 2.4 GHz wireless connectivity solution. Bluetooth supports data transmissions between devices of up to 721 Kbps and up to three voice channels.

Bluetooth is designed for wireless PANs for data exchange between devices such as desktop computers, notebooks, pocket computers, cameras, printers, mobile phones, fax machines, etc. It is supported by companies including Ericcson, IBM, Intel, Nokia, and Toshiba.

King Harald Bluetooth

Harald Bluetooth (910–987) was the first Christian king of Denmark. He united Denmark under his rule in the mid-900s. Bluetooth comes from two Danish words, Blå (meaning dark complexion) and tan (meaning great man).

Harald inherited the kingdom of Denmark from his father, Gorm the Old, in about 958. His base of power was at Jelling, near present-day Vejle. Harald continued his father's efforts to expand the kingdom and to bring all of it more tightly under royal authority. Harald built many fortresses, roads, and bridges. He also defended Denmark from attacks by the Germans to the south. In about 960, Harold converted to Christianity. He encouraged the spread of Christianity in Denmark and built a number of churches.

In the late 950s and 960s, Harald twice helped Norwegian rebels overthrow their King. Harald later claimed the title King of Norway, though he never controlled more than a small area in southeastern Norway.

In the mid-980s, Harald's son Sweyn rebelled against him. Harald was forced to flee Denmark and died in about 987. Sweyn, later known as Sweyn Forkbeard, became king.

Most of the Harald's history was preserved on two runic stones erected to his memory in Jelling, Denmark.

Bluetooth technology created in Lund, Sweden by Ericsson bears the name of this famous forefather. Ericsoon has even erected a modern runic stone to the memory of Harald Bluetooth.

Why Choose Bluetooth?

- Reliable
- Flexible
- No cables or wires
- Mobile
- Low cost
- Support from big companies
- Support from the handheld-devices industry

Why Not Choose Bluetooth?

- Limited range
- Slow data-transmission rate
- Devices must have a Bluetooth chip

Wired Networks

The majority of all networks in the world today are created using wires. Perhaps the most notable of all of these networks is the Internet. There really is not anything fancy or different about how the Internet is designed. A wired network in your home would look like a small scale model of the Internet.

Chapter 3 will discuss wiring your home network, should you choose a wired network. Wiring a network is the only significant disadvantage this type of network has when considered against other network technologies. This chapter discusses some interesting alternatives to complicated wiring, such as the first type of network described that uses your existing phone lines.

Home Phone Lines

Phones have been in homes for decades. Historically, a home would only have one phone. Today, it is typical to have a phone jack in almost every room. This means that the phone lines running throughout your house are completely interconnected and form a network. The telephone wire in your home is sufficient to carry data at pretty fast speeds.

The most important thing to know about networking over your home phone lines is that your computer network will not interfere with your phone services. You could talk on the phone or use your fax machine while the computers remain connected. The data from the computers and voice (or fax) are carried on different frequencies (see Figure 2.1).

The Home Phoneline Networking Alliance, an industry group, created a standard named after their alliance, HomePNA. The two current HomePNA standards offer the following bandwidths:

- HomePNA 1.0 – 1 Mbps
- HomePNA 2.0 – 10 Mbps

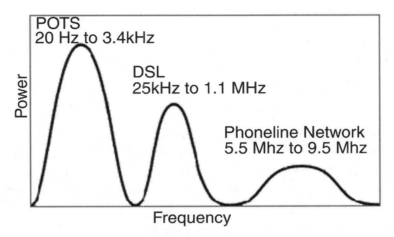

Figure 2.1 *Information traveling across a phone line does not interfere when it is transmitted at different frequencies.*

HomePNA uses Frequency Division Multiplexing (FDM) which divides the phone or frequencies for the phone line to carry different services. Because they use different frequencies, they do not interfere with each other. In Figure 2.1 you first see the protocol that handles audio signals from a traditional telephone, called POTS (Plain Old Telephone Service). The signal used to transfer data over a DSL line is at a higher frequency. Then, at an even higher frequency, you have HomePNA.

Most homes in the Unites States are able to use HomePNA technology, as long as the home has a phone line and more than one phone jack. The network can support up to 25 devices which can be placed up to 500 feet apart in homes up to 10,000 square feet. Some of the different devices that can be connected to your network are

- Printers
- Scanners
- Cameras
- Webcams
- PCs
- Macintosh computers

- Laptops
- Telephones
- Webphones
- TVs (set-top box)
- Others

HomePNA connects all of the computers around the house to the network. Everyone in the network can access the Internet simultaneously and share files. When using ADSL or a cable modem, family members can talk on the phone, browse the Internet, play network games, print, or share files with other computers on the network.

There is no need for new wires around your home. All of the wires are in place already. Depending on the quality of the wiring in your home, your network can have a high-speed LAN connectivity, up to 10 Mbps.

HomePNA works with Macs and older PCs and is compatible with other home-networking technologies such as ethernet and wireless types. It is also compatible with high-speed Internet access such as DSL and cable. HomePNA does not require a hub, category 5 (CAT5) wiring, filters, or splitters (sometimes used for devices such as DSL modems).

Why Choose HomePNA?

- Inexpensive
- Easy to install because it uses the existing phone wire
- Standardized
- Reliable
- Easy to reconfigure your home network without rewiring
- Fast data transmission up to 10 Mbps
- Operates at 10 Mbps, even if phone is in use
- Does not require an access point (hub or router)
- Supports up to 25 devices
- Compatible with other network technologies

Why Not Choose HomePNA?

- Limited speed compared to other wired or even wireless networks
- Not really an industry-standard networking technology

Power Lines

Another interesting solution to the problem of having to run cables around your house is to use the ac electric wires. The same wires that carry the 110 volts to power your computer can also carry network signals. There is no investment in cables or time spent having to wire your house. Anywhere there is an ac outlet, you have a potential network. The idea is identical to the phoneline networks. Any wire that continuously runs throughout your house can be used as a network. The ac ground wire is continuous, even when switches and circuit breakers are turned off.

Powerline networks are the slowest home networks on the market. When a 1 Mbps speed is advertised, be aware that this is best-case speed, and that normal noise on your home's electric wiring will cause the network to run slower. Older homes tend to have more noise on the electric wiring. There are some solutions now available for this unique type of network. For example, a large telecommunications company called Nortel has a product called the DPL 1000 that uses Digital Powerline® technology to transmit data at 1 Mbps.

 Warning! You may have security problems when using powerline networks in an apartment building. It is possible that your network traffic will be available to other powerline network users in the same building.

Powerline networks use a protocol called Frequency Shift Keying (FSK) to transmit data using two frequencies that are far above the normal 60Hz ac electricity traveling across the same wire.

Why Choose Powerline Networking?

- Low cost
- Easy installation
- More possible network connection points than phoneline networks

Why Not Choose Powerline Networking?

• Extremely slow data transfer rates

• Poor security

• Not much industry support

Ethernet

Ethernet is the most common LAN protocol in use. There are two primary varieties of ethernet networks, 100 Mb (100baseT) and the older 10 Mb (10baseT). One of the things that makes ethernet so popular is the way computers interconnect. On an ethernet network, each computer (known as a *station*) operates independently from all of the other computers on the network. There is no central controller for the network. Without a central controller, if one computer on the network is turned off or is disabled, the other computers can continue to function and communicate over the network.

A Little Ethernet Background

Some people think that connecting printers to a network is a great "side" benefit of computer networking. A little known fact is that sharing printers was the primary impetus for inventing networks in the first place. Bob Metcalfe, one of the inventors of ethernet, was originally tasked by his employer, Xerox Palo Alto Research Center (PARC), to network the computers together so they could use their newest invention, the laser printer.

Metcalfe first conceived of ethernet after reading a paper by Dr. Norman Abramson who was also working on the Palo Alto ALOHANET at the University of Hawaii. ALOHANET is considered the world's first modern data network, operating at 9600 bps broadcasting packets of data throughout the State of Hawaii.

ALOHANET had an efficiency limit due to network collisions and consequential loss of packets to "the ether". In his computer science thesis, Abramson attempted to solve network collision of packets and data loss. In the mid to late 1970s, applying his work at PARC, he patented a "Multipoint data communication system with collision detection" along with Boggs, Thacker and Lampson, members of his PARC Place team. Ethernet is now the most common networking technology.

When choosing a network, you need to understand just a little about how an ethernet network gets its cryptic name (10baseT or 100baseT). Ethernet networks have a designation that is made up of three parts. The first, numeric part is the speed of the network. In most cases this is either going to be a 10 for 10 Mb/second or 100 for 100 Mb/second. The second part, *base*, stands for baseband (not important). The third part of the designation gives you a rough idea of how long the cable can be (segment length) measured in meters (a meter is a little over a yard). If the third part is a letter, it stands for the type of cable used.

The following are some examples:

- 5 – Thick coaxial cable, 500-meter segment length,
  (about three football fields)
- 2 – Thin coaxial cable, 185-meter segment length (rounded up)
- T – Twisted pair (two wires twisted together)
- F – Fiber optic, glass fiber cable

The following is a discussion of the two most common types of ethernet networks.

10baseT

The 10 Mb twisted pair ethernet network is the most commonly used network. It is simple and inexpensive to create using wire similar to your home telephone wire. A 10baseT network only requires two wires—one to send data and the other to receive data. Most of the wired networking hardware you will find in stores is either 10baseT or 100baseT, which is discussed in the next section.

Why Choose 10baseT?

- Fast enough for any home application
- Inexpensive
- Reliable
- Most widely used network on the planet
- Pretty easy to install

- If you need help, you are most likely to find someone who can help you with this type of network
- Works on both Macintosh and Windows-running computers (In fact, almost every computer in the world can use this type of network.)

Why Not Choose 10baseT?

- Computer applications now require more bandwidth. Your home network may "bog down" while several different people in the home attempt to video conference, print, and download music simultaneously.
- Newer technology now exists for nearly the same price. It is likely that 10baseT home products will eventually become obsolete.
- Even though broadband Internet connections are currently only a tenth of the speed of 10baseT, Internet connectivity is also changing to allow for greater bandwidth. You do not want your home network to end up slower than your Internet connection.

100baseT

This network is ten times faster than 10baseT, and 10 times faster than almost every other type of network on the market. It costs just a few dollars more to install this type of network, but the benefits far outweigh the cost of installing 100baseT instead of 10baseT.

Most Internet access is slow compared to the speeds of most LANs. Some of the fastest Internet access you can get at home is around 1.5 Mbps. So, Internet access is not the reason to install 100baseT. Even with several people on your network at the same time trying to use the Internet, the speed of the connection will only be as fast as the link you establish, no matter what type of modem it is.

The reason to install 100baseT, if you decide to install a wired network, is the future—not the distant future, but the next five years. The number of home appliances that will be attached to your network and the amount of information that will be shared just inside your home, without taking the Internet into account, is going to grow at an astronomical rate. You should be prepared for the time when nearly everything in your house is networked. It is not a simple thing to install network cable, but it is true that the network cable you install for 100baseT will also work for 10baseT. In fact, in Chapter 3 we discuss options for slowly migrating from 10baseT to 100baseT.

Why Choose 100baseT?

- 100 times faster than nearly every other type of home network
- Sufficient bandwidth for all home network requirements, today and in the near future
- Same installation requirements as 10baseT; easy to upgrade from 10baseT to 100baseT
- Standardized equipment
- Fairly inexpensive

Why Not Choose 100baseT?

Many network products allow both 10baseT and 100baseT traffic as people transition between technologies. If you have equipment that currently operates as 10baseT you may choose to standardize your network on 10baseT. This decision will likely hold you in good stead for several years.

USB and Firewire

USB and firewire are two similar technologies in use today in most new computers. These technologies were designed to make it easier to plug peripheral devices into your computer. Not only that, but computers were running out of serial ports, and a new technology was needed to expand the ability of computers to have more things attached. It only makes sense that networks would make use of these ports.

USB

The USB (Universal Serial Bus) port that comes standard in most PCs today replaces many uses of the older serial port of the computer. One of the first ways to interconnect computers was to string a cable between the serial ports of the computer and use serial communications to communicate. Modems, connected to a serial port, are simply devices that allow computers to send serial communications over a telephone line. Computers connected directly using a cable do not require the special electronic noises created by a modem to send their signals to each other.

One of the main advantages of USB is that it is 100 times faster than a standard serial port. Also, a normal serial port can only have a single device attached, whereas USB allows a computer to have as many as 127 devices connected using multiple USB ports.

Unlike the older serial port, you cannot simply connect two computers together using a cable. You need a USB bridge, or special USB network adapters.

Warning! Connecting two USB ports together using a standard USB cable is an electrical hazard and may cause serious damage to both computers!

We should mention here that even though USB is very compatible—supported by all versions of Windows from Windows 98 and greater and by Macintosh computers running Macintosh OS 8.5 and greater—it was not really designed to operate as a LAN. If you are simply connecting two or three computers that you do not expect to transmit much data, you might consider this option. Otherwise, the organization that assists in establishing the USB standard, the USB Implementers Forum, Inc (*http://www.usb.org*) does not recommend that you network computers using USB.

One USB product that lets two Windows computers communicate is the ActionTec ActionLink USB Cable Room-to-Room Starter kit (*http://www.actiontec.com*). With this product, your two computers must virtually be in the same room, as the maximum distance between the computers can only be 20 feet.

A more powerful alternative allows you to network as many as 17 computers using the USB port. The EZ-Link Instant Network (*http://www.ezlinkusb.com*) allows you to connect computers in a daisy chain, star configuration, or a combination of both configurations. The specification for this network is a data rate of about 4 Mbps.

Note: Using USB networks you sacrifice speed for simplicity. Standard, inexpensive ethernet systems operate at 10 Mbps, more than twice the rated speed of the EZ-Link system.

Why Choose USB?

- You are dead set against opening your computer, or letting anyone else open your computer
- Simple to install—simply plug it into your USB port, and configure the software
- Could be great for plugging two computers in the same room together

Why Not Choose USB?

- Tends to be slower than other types of networks
- Not very expandable—the distance between computers is very small, so they tend to be used for networking computers in the same room

Firewire

A competitor to USB was developed by Apple Computers and is called *firewire*. You may occasionally hear it referred to by its more technical designation: IEEE 1394. It is faster than USB, and there is some indication in the industry that it just may replace USB as a means to connect peripherals to computers.

Technical Note: Firewire is not just for Apple Macintosh computers. There are now firewire adapters for PCs. If you happen to be running Windows ME, installing a firewire adapter also installs a virtual network adapter. This network adapter can be configured for networking. Windows ME uses a standard called "IP over IEEE 1394 (Internet RFC 2734)."

Want a home network that blows away most top-of-the-line 100 Mb networks? FireNet, by Unibrain (*http://www.unibrain.com*) has a network speed of 400 Mbps. This product is supported on both Windows-running and Macintosh computers.

Most homes will not have two types of networks, but in case you and your kids have switched from Tinker Toys® to building networks, you will be happy to know that firewire networks can be interconnected to standard ethernet networks simply by having a machine with both types of adapters act as a bridge between the two types of networks.

Not so Technical Note: Tinker Toys®, invented by Pajeau in 1914, are still enjoyed by children today.

Why Choose Firewire?

- Very easy to install
- Some are extremely fast
- Most are compatible with and can be interconnected to ethernet networks

Why Not Choose Firewire?

- Support for this networking technology is limited

Summary

Performance is what you should care about most when selecting a network. Some technologies, such as the wireless networks, are more expensive, and this may be an important factor. For the most part, though, what you want most from a network is that it does its job reliably and fast enough to meet your needs.

Following the basic information in this chapter you should be able to make an informed decision about the type of network you would like to install. On the other hand, you may still be uncertain of which technology you would prefer. In that case, the following chapters of this book that discuss installation of the hardware and software may help you decide which network installation you would like to tackle.

Remember, there are always network professionals who would happily install your network for you. Do not feel that it is something you have to do yourself. They may even offer you advice beyond what is offered in this book or provide newer information than what was available when we wrote this book. It pays be to be current and informed.

Setting up the Hardware 3

Chapter 2 discussed selecting the type of network that would best meet your needs. Depending on the type of network you choose to install, you may need different types of cable, network adapters, hubs, routers, radio receivers, and more. This chapter helps you figure out what kind of hardware you need and how to set it up.

Cables and Wires

The types of cables you need to create a network, and whether you even need cables at all, depends on the type of network you choose. Use the following sections as a guide to help you choose and install the right equipment.

Standard Network Cables

Ethernet networks are the most commonly installed networks. Therefore, it should be no surprise that the most common network cable used today is the type used in ethernet networks such as 10baseT, 100baseT, and even the experimental 1000baseT. There are four types of cable used for ethernet.

- Unshielded Twisted Pair (UTP)
- Shielded Twisted Pair (STP)
- Fiber optic cable
- Coaxial cable (Coax)

UTP (Figure 3.1) is the most common type of network cable because of its low price and versatility. STP includes a special foil shield around the twisted-pair wires to protect them from Electro-Magnetic Interference (EMI). It is more expensive and not absolutely necessary in home networks. Fiber optic cable is still very expensive but is being used more for fast network types such as the gigabit/second Asynchronous Transfer Mode (ATM) networks. Coaxial cable, once the only type of network cable, is rarely used today. It is thick, expensive, and used primarily to form networks in a ring pattern, rather than the popular star pattern.

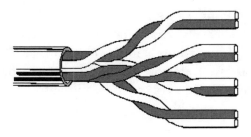

Figure 3.1 *Wires twisted together aid in signal strength.*

Twisted-pair cables are rated for data throughput and given a rating called a category. There are more categories than those listed, but here are the ones that apply to home networking:

- Category 3 – Data speeds up to 16 Mhz with a throughput rate up to 10 Mbps
- Category 4 – Data speeds up to 20 Mhz with a throughput rate up to 16 Mbps
- Category 5 – Data speeds up to 100 Mhz with a throughput rate up to 100 Mbps*

* *Category 5 is being used at higher bandwidths and speed experimentally. Categories 6 and 7 are under development at this time.*

The most commonly used cable type is Category 5, sometimes abbreviated to cat 5. You can purchase network cables, with nicely molded plastic connectors and cut to specific lengths, in most electronic parts and consumer electronics stores. The package will normally identify the cable as cat 5 and compatible with 10baseT or both 10baseT and 100baseT networks. These pre-cut lengths of cable are also known as *whips*.

Crossover Cables

When connecting two hubs, some types of cable and DSL modems, or other devices with ports wired identically, you need a special cable, wired differently from the typical straight-through network cable. The wires in a crossover cable are wired according to the pinout in Table 3.3. This enables the data send port of the first network device to communicate with the data receive port on the second network device.

If you are trying to connect your laptop to a network hub, some PCMCIA network cards have specially attached network cables that normally plug directly into the hub. If your hub is in the bedroom closet, this could be very inconvenient. You can use a crossover cable and a two-sided female connector to make an extension allowing you to use your laptop in other, possibly more convenient, locations in your home.

Making Your Own Cable

When creating a network in your home, often it is not feasible to purchase a network cable long enough to reach computers all over the house. When this happens, it is just as easy to make your own cable.

What You Need

Making your own cables is not difficult. You just need to purchase the right equipment. Most importantly you will need a crimp tool (Figure 3.2) for fastening the wires into male RJ45 connectors, as shown in Figure 3.3.

You can purchase RJ45 crimpers in many electronic stores, though you may not find them in the same consumer electronics stores where you purchase your other network hardware. These crimpers can also be used to create RJ11 (telephone) jacks for creating your own telephone cables.

The crimper serves two purposes. First, the wire trimmer/stripper helps you trim away the insulation from the cable jacket and, second, it has a guide that lets you trim the exposed conductors to the correct length.

Next you will need to purchase RJ45 male connectors. These are the plastic ends similar to the ones that modular telephone jacks accept (RJ11), except that they are bigger and have twice as many pins (Figure 3.3). Most Radio Shack stores or other electronics stores carry these connectors in bulk.

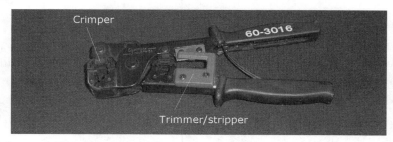

Figure 3.2 *You will need an RJ45 crimp tool.*

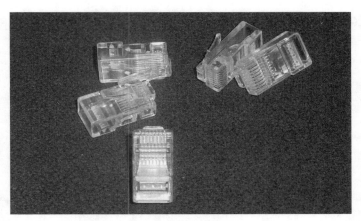

Figure 3.3 *You need two RJ45 connectors per cable.*

Tip: Buy more connectors than you need. It takes practice to make a perfect network connection. Also, you never know when you might want to make another network cable.

Cat 5 Cable

Cat 5 cable normally has eight conductors (wires) housed in a single jacket (insulator) and if the wires are shielded, there is a thin layer of foil just under the jacket completely surrounding the eight wires. There are four pairs of wire, twisted in a pattern to increase signal strength. Believe it or not, the number of twists per inch actually makes a difference in the performance of the cable.

Cutting the Cable

Keep each cable length under 295 feet in length. The longer you make the cable, the slower the response time over the network. Lengths longer than 295 feet are outside the limits of an ethernet cable and will cause data errors.

When trimming away the insulation to expose the wires in the cable, try to keep the wires twisted as pairs as close to the ends as possible, at least up to about a half inch from the end.

Table 3.1 shows you the color codes of a standard, straight-through connection according to the industry standard. It is important to know a couple things at this point. Your cable may not have these colors! It does not matter what color the wires are. What matters is that you pair the wires according to the diagram.

Table 3.1 Four-Pair Cable Pinout (EIA/TIA 568B standard color scheme)

Function/Name	Pin #	Color Code	Pin #	Function/Name
Transmit TX+	1	White/Orange	1	TX+
Transmit TX−	2	Orange	2	TX−
Receive RX+	3	White/Green	3	RX+
	4	Blue	4	
	5	White/Blue	5	
Receive RX−	6	Green	6	RX−
	7	White/Brown	7	
	8	Brown	8	

Note: Keep each pair of wires as a pair. TX+ and TX− must be paired and RX+ and RX− must also be paired.

As mentioned in the Note, the wires in your network cable used for pins 1 and 2 and pins 3 and 6 must be from the same twisted pairs. Also, make sure you document which colors you used in which pins so you use the same color pattern on the other end. If you forget to write them down, it is sometimes very difficult to tell after you have crimped the wires into the connector. Table 3.2 simplifies the pairing for you. Remember, do not worry about the color issue.

Table 3.2 Pins by Color Pairing

Pair Number	Pins	Common Color
1	4 and 5	Blue
2	1 and 2	Orange
3	3 and 6	Green
4	7 and 8	Brown

Strip the outside jacket away from the inside wires using the trimmer on the handle of your crimp tool. You can also carefully use a razor knife or other wire-stripping tool. The trick here is to cut it away without damaging any of the internal wires. If you knick a wire, cut the cable and start over again.

Once you have stripped away the insulation and trimmed the wires using the guided trimmer on the crimp tool, trim both ends of the cable, and remember, keep the wires twisted as much as possible.

Take the cable end to which you are going to attach a connector, and straighten the wire ends so they align with the pins in the connector. The straighter you make these ends, aligned flat, the easier it will be to make a good connection.

Note: You should not remove the insulation from the wire ends. The plastic RJ45 connector will insert a metal probe through the plastic insulation into the wire making a connection. This metal probe through the insulation also serves to anchor the wire to the connector.

Hold the RJ45 connector in one hand with the plastic retaining clip held up (Figure 3.4), carefully insert the wires into the back of the clip as shown. Each wire should fit into the small plastic channel within the connector. Visually inspect the connector to see that all of the wires have been fully inserted. You may have to pull the wires out and try this more than once. Two things to pay attention to are that the wires are in the right channel and that the wires are fully inserted. The hard part is over.

Gently place the RJ45 connector, with the wires inserted, into the crimping slot on the end of the crimp tool, and crimp firmly. Two actions take place when crimping the connector. The first thing that happens is that the plastic channels are compressed, forcing the metal pins through the plastic insulation, making electrical contact with the wires. The second thing that takes place is that the cable itself is compressed in a plastic cable clamp on the end of the connector. If you have trimmed your wires too long, this cable clamp may not fasten the cable firmly to the connector. This is not the end of the world, but is less than optimal. Care should be taken handling a connector that has not been crimped to the insulation (jacket) of the network cable. Repeat this process for both ends of the cable.

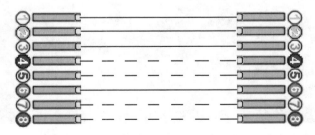

Figure 3.4 *Pins 1 2 ,3 and 6 are required, the others, shown as dashed lines, are optional.*

Tip: To make a crossover cable, simply follow the pinout in Table 3.3.

Table 3.3 Crossover Pinout for 10/100baseT Cables

Connector One	Connector Two
1	3
2	6
3	1
6	2

Checking Your Cables

It is important to test your new cables. Even manufactured cables purchased from the store can be bad, or can go bad over time with hard use. One quick test of the cable is to plug a known, working network card into a working hub. The status light should indicate that a good connection has been made. This is not a certain indication, however, that all is well with the cable. Only later, after you have configured your computer software and expect a network connection, will you be sure if your cable is working.

Another way to test your cable involves purchasing an inexpensive, but very useful piece of test equipment. A tone generator (shown in Figure 3.5) is an invaluable tool. This tool allows you to test each pair by generating a tone on each pair of wires. Using a separate tone probe (normally sold together) you can test the other end of the cable to see if the tone is present, and present on the pin where it is expected. It is easy to inadvertantly miswire a cable. It pays to be careful, and it helps to have this tool or know someone who has one you can borrow.

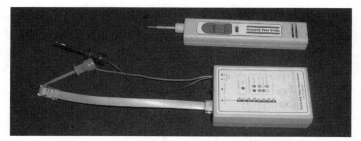

Figure 3.5 *An optional tone generator will help you test or troubleshoot your cables.*

Network Interface Cards

Computers have a motherboard that forms the heart of your computer. In addition, different types of computer cards are plugged into your computer that give it additional abilities, such as video cards that allow you to attach a monitor.

Most networks, with a couple of exceptions like USB and firewire networks, require your computer to have a Network Interface Card (NIC). These are sometimes simply known as network cards or network adapters. These either plug into your computer's motherboard expansion slots, or in the case of computers that use the small PCMCIA cards (PC Cards), such as laptop computers, they may simply plug into the PC card slot.

Note: Macintosh computers come with NICs installed that are compatible with creating an ethernet network.

PCI vs. ISA

Before purchasing a NIC, you will need to know what type of expansion slot you have available in your computer. When we refer to expansion slots, we are referring to the card-edge connectors located on your computer's motherboard. There are two types—Industry Standard Architecture (ISA) and Peripheral Component Interconnect (PCI). ISA expansion slots are an older and slower technology, being slowly replaced by PCI expansion slots. ISA slots are included in computers today only for backward compatibility with existing cards. Your computer may not come equipped with ISA slots.

To determine which type of expansion slot you have available in your computer, you will need to open your computer. Follow the directions in the following section carefully.

Opening the Computer

Warning! Follow these steps and suggestions carefully. There is an electric shock hazard when working on electric equipment.

These instructions are generic to most PC computer systems. Your computer may be different. Because most Apple computers come with network cards preinstalled, these instructions refer to Windows PC computers.

Carefully follow these steps:

1. Close all running programs and choose Shutdown from the Start menu. When asked if you want to Shutdown or Restart, select Shutdown. Then wait until your computer tells you it is OK to shut off your computer.

2. Once you are told that it is safe to turn off your computer, locate the power switch on your computer, and turn off the power. The power switch on most newer computers is located on the front of the computer. If not, you will find it on the back. Also, some newer computers have a safety feature that requires you to hold the power button down for three or more seconds before the computer will shut off.

3. Look at the back of the computer, and UNPLUG THE POWER CORD! We cannot stress this enough. Removing the power cord is the only way to ensure that there is no chance of electric shock. The power cord is usually black, and has a rectangular plug into the back of your computer. To be certain you are unplugging the correct cable, you can follow the plug to the wall socket or surge protector.

4. (Optional) If you feel confident unplugging the monitor, keyboard, mouse, and any printer cables, you might want to do that at this time so you can move the computer to a more comfortable place to work.

5. In this next step, you might want to refer to the manual that came with your computer. Each computer case is slightly different, and instructions for opening the case are unique to each type and brand of case. Most computer cases will open after removing the screws in the back of the case. These are normally Philips head screws and sometimes have a hex head for use with a nut driver or socket. Once these screws are removed, lift the case away from the computer. (Remember, these instructions could be different for your computer. Some tower computer cases, for example, are equipped with side doors that are easily opened. Follow the first three steps even if opening the side door is simple.)

6. Locate the motherboard of your computer (Figure 3.6).

7. Locate any free expansion slots on the motherboard. If your computer has both ISA and PCI slots available, your preference will be PCI when purchasing a network card. PCI slots will appear smaller than ISA slots, and the connector pins are more numerous and narrow (Figure 3.7).

Figure 3.6 *The motherboard is the main board of your computer.*

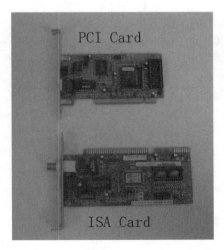

Figure 3.7 *A PCI card looks physically different from an ISA style network card.*

Chances are good that you will have a free PCI slot in your computer. If you do not have a free PCI slot, but have a free ISA slot, you will need to purchase a network card compatible with ISA. Otherwise, you will need to purchase a PCI compatible network card.

You will need to repeat these steps for each computer you would like to add to the network. It is not necessary for all of your computers to have identical network cards. If you purchase a kit, explained later in this chapter, you will need to be certain that you have the correct expansion slots available in each computer—compatible with those sold in the kit.

At the Store

You will need an NIC for each computer you are including in your network. Any other network-ready devices and appliances you would like to include on your network will most likely already have an NIC preinstalled.

Once you have decided on what type of network you want to install in your home, it is a good idea to shop for good bargains. You can find networking hardware at most large office supply stores, many large consumer electronics stores, and, of course, computer stores.

Buying name-brand components is not always the most important consideration when purchasing computers and components, but in this case it is. Other generic or off-brand network cards may perform as well as those having a name brand. Your main consideration in this case is not the hardware—it is the software that comes with it, commonly known as the *drivers*. We discuss drivers in more detail in Chapter 5.

As new versions of computer operating systems are released, you want to be certain that drivers are available for your NIC. If the company that made your card no longer exists, or no longer makes network cards, you could be out of luck and have to purchase a new network card simply because the software of your old card is no longer supported. This is generally not a problem with well-known network equipment makers such as 3Com, Linksys, and D-Link. The equipment from these manufacturers is reliable and well supported.

Selecting an Ethernet Network Interface Card

Chapter 2 introduced the two primary types of ethernet networks, 10baseT and 100baseT. You should know which type of NIC you want to purchase based on the speed of the network you have selected.

There are three basic types of ethernet NICs available in most stores, or online:

- 10baseT – 10 Mbps twisted pair
- 100baseT – 100 Mbps twisted pair
- Combo Card – Capable of supporting both 10 Mbps and 100 Mbps over twisted pair

The 10baseT cards are readily available, and pretty inexpensive. Their lower cost is partially due to the fact that most people are installing fast ethernet cards (100baseT). Unless you already own a 10baseT network, or expect to use your computer on someone else's 10baseT network, the only reason to purchase this slower card is price.

Note: You may want to keep in mind that saving money today may cost you more in the future. Eventually 10baseT cards will be phased out and replaced with the faster 100baseT, or possibly faster network types.

The 100baseT cards are recommended. They may cost a little more, but as the Internet adopts more multimedia applications and computers evolve further as communication and entertainment devices, you will be happy you have the extra bandwidth provided by these faster network cards on your LAN.

Combo cards are NICs that support both 10baseT and 100baseT. Most combo cards can sense the type of network in which they have been installed, and switch to the correct operating speed. The following are some reasons you may want to purchase a combo card:

- You have a 10baseT network now, or are purchasing a 10baseT network, and believe that at some point you will change to a 100baseT network. Choosing a combo card will save you money in the future because you will not need to purchase new network cards.
- You operate your computer, such as your laptop, on different computer networks, and wish to be able to plug into both 10baseT and 100baseT networks.

Note: If you are currently using either a DSL modem or cable modem to connect to the Internet, you probably already have an NIC installed in your computer. Chances are good that it is a 10baseT NIC, because cable and DSL modems currently do not support fast ethernet.

Installing a Network Interface Card

If you have not already powered down your computer and opened the case, follow the directions in the Opening the Computer section earlier in this chapter.

Locate the empty expansion port and carefully move any wires away from the area. There should be a small metal cover plate (Figure 3.8) next to the expansion port. This cover plate should now be removed. To remove the cover plate, remove the retaining screw (Figure 3.9), using a Philips-head screwdriver. Carefully remove the screw so that it does not fall down inside the computer case. Screws can sometimes become lodged under the motherboard, and if not removed, can cause an electrical short circuit, ruining the motherboard. Some cover plates are connected to the frame with a small metal tab. Disconnect the cover plate by wiggling it back and forth until it is free of the frame, breaking the metal connection tab.

Tip: On some computer cases, the temporary metal cover plate is punched out incompletely, and must be removed with a light twisting motion to break the metal connection to the case.

Figure 3.8 *Remove the cover plate before inserting the network card.*

Figure 3.9 *Remove the retaining screw from the top of the cover plate.*

For this next step, it is recommended that you wear a grounding strap to eliminate the possibility of static discharge into the sensitive electronic circuitry. Inexpensive straps, even disposable straps, are available at most computer and electronics stores. If you choose not to wear a strap, try to ground yourself before handling the card by touching something metal, or at least the computer case.

Remove the NIC from its protective antistatic wrapper, and insert the card into the selected expansion slot, making certain the card is properly seated. Reinsert the Philips screw that once held the temporary metal plate. This will hold your network card in place. Before tightening this screw, look along the back of your computer to make certain that none of the case is blocking the RJ45 jacks in the network card. You can adjust the position of the card from side to side before tightening this screw. Notice the positioning in Figure 3.10 where only a network card has been installed in a PCI slot.

Replace the cover on your computer case and refasten any retaining screws or latches. You may now reconnect the power cord and any other cables you may have disconnected when opening the case. When you have completed reassembling your computer, turn it on.

Figure 3.10 *This combo 10/100 card has been inserted in a PCI slot above the darker ISA slots.*

Your computer should sense that a new piece of hardware is installed using its plug-and-play feature, and attempt to install drivers for the new network card. Follow any instructions that came with your network card for driver installation. Your network card may or may not have come with its own software drivers. Windows 98 and greater have most of the drivers necessary available on the operating system's installation disk or CD-ROM. We will cover software installation in greater detail in Chapter 5.

Hubs

Ethernet networks, whether wired or wireless, normally require hubs. These are pieces of equipment to which each of your computers on the network are connected either by cable or some wireless link. Since ethernet networks are configured in a star pattern, where the hub sits at the center of the star.

Wired Hubs

The most common type of network hub, currently, is an ethernet hub that accepts network cable connections from your computer. When you check your local store's networking hardware shelf, the Ethernet hub is the type you are most likely to find due to its overwhelming popularity.

Just like ethernet NICs, hubs come in three basic varieties: 10baseT, 100baseT, and combo hubs that support both speeds (Figure 3.11).

Today, most 100baseT hubs support a combination of 10baseT and 100baseT connections. In fact, most 100baseT hubs simply sense the type of NIC attached to them and adjust the speed accordingly. If you have a combo NIC connected to a 100baseT hub, the hub and card will operate at the fastest available speed.

One reason why you will need a hub that supports both 10baseT as well as 100baseT is that chances are good that you will need to plug network devices other than your computer into the hub. For example, if you are using an external DSL modem or cable modem to connect to the Internet, you can plug it directly into the network hub, sharing it with all of the other computers on the network. (See the Note about network cards and cable or DSL modems on page 44.) Using a dual speed hub allows you to enjoy faster speeds between devices on your LAN, and also prepares your network for the eventual increase in broadband modem speeds.

Figure 3.11 *Linksys Etherfast® 10/100 5-Port Workgroup Switch is an example of an ethernet hub.*

Selecting a Hub

There are only two technical considerations when buying a hub—speed (10 or 100 Mbps) and how many ports with which the hub is equipped. A port is the RJ45 socket (see cabling information in the What You'll Need section in Chapter 4) that allows you to plug in a standard network cable.

As mentioned previously, most 100baseT ethernet hubs will also support 10baseT "automagically." They sense the type of card installed in your computer and adjust the speed accordingly. This is true for most 100baseT Ethernet hubs but not all. The most important thing you can do when purchasing a hub is to carefully read the box!

Because hubs do not require software to be installed on your computer, there is no worry about drivers, and thus no worry about which brand of hub to buy. Of course, the old adage of "you get what you pay for" still holds true. As long as you purchase a hub that is technically capable of supporting your NIC, it is not necessary that the brand of card match the brand of hub.

Another important consideration in selecting a hub is choosing the number of ports the hub supports. There are two kinds of ports:

- Standard data port
- Crossover port

Standard data cables are used to connect your computer, via a network cable, to the hub. The hub performs a crossover internally, so that the SEND (aka TRANSMIT) signal is sent to from the hub to a receive port on another computer. Crossover ports are used to connect hubs to other hubs and to some types of DSL and cable modems. They are called crossover ports for a single reason—they undo the automatic crossover normally done by the hub, and allow SEND and RECEIVE signals to continue on unobstructed to the corresponding SEND and RECEIVE ports of the next hub.

Note: The crossover port on your hub may have a fancy name, such as "uplink port," and may not be referred to as a crossover port.

Using either a crossover port or a crossover cable, you can connect one network hub to another, increasing the number of ports available to your network. Network hubs come standard with as few as four ports, and configurations that have as many as 24 ports in a single hub. Most hubs found in the store are five-port hubs, sufficient for most home applications.

You need a port for each computer you are connecting to the network. One port will be the crossover port and will not be useable for connecting a computer to the hub. If you are connecting a DSL or cable modem to your network, that will also require a port.

Chapter 8 describes some of the other types of equipment you may want to include in your network, such as network printers and network hard drives. When calculating the number of ports you need, be sure to keep these in mind, or any future needs for which you may want to plan. Of course, you will also have to keep your budget in mind. Five-port hubs generally cost less then $100 and costs increase substantially as you increase the number of ports.

Connecting a Hub

Placement of your hub is one of the more important considerations. Here are some things to think about when choosing a place for your hub:

- There needs to be an ac outlet to provide power to your hub. (See Tip about power backup below.)
- Each computer is going to run a cable to your hub, so the location should be convenient to accept multiple cables.
- The hub should be located in a cool, dry place away from heavy machinery or powerful motors.
- For ease of troubleshooting, place your hub where you can easily view the front panel status lights.

 Tip: If your computers are protected from power outage using an Uninterruptable Power Supply (UPS), which is strongly recommended, you should also plug your network hub's ac plug into the UPS.

Once you have found a permanent location for your network hub, you can choose to set it on a shelf, or mount it to a wall, shelf, or even a rack specially designed for mounting computer hardware—some hubs have the mounting hardware necessary for these arrangements. Rack-mounted hardware is probably not appropriate for most home applications.

Connect computers to the hub by plugging the RJ45 connectors into the ports found on either the front or back of your hub. If the other end of the network cable is connected to a network card installed in a running computer, you should see a network status light illuminate when you plug in the cable. Most hubs have small numbered LEDs on the front face of the hub. When a proper, physical network connection is made to the hub, the light should be green. Otherwise, it may appear red or dark.

The network status light is one of the simplest ways to know when you have a valid connection. Some 100baseT hubs have different indicator lights depending on whether the connection is made to a 10baseT or a 100baseT interface card.

Many NICs also have status lights. You should see those LEDs turn on when the connection is made. Combo cards often have different status lights depending on whether they are connected to a 10baseT or a 100baseT hub.

Note: It is not necessary to power down either the computer or the hub when plugging or unplugging network cables.

Phone-Line Connections

As discussed in Chapter 2, you can use your home phone line to create a network connection. Operating at a frequency that ranges between 5.5 MHz and 9.5 MHz, these networks will not interfere with your normal telephone conversations that usually operate at frequencies in the kHz instead of MHz bandwidth or with xDSL services.

The three brands of home phoneline networks currently available are Intel's AnyPoint, Diamond's HomeFree, and the LinkSys Homelink.

The 1 Mbps and 10 Mbps home phoneline networks come with a variety of connection possibilities including

- Parallel port – Only for 1 Mbps network connections
- USB port – For both 1 Mbps and 10 Mbps connections
- PCI card – For both 1 Mbps and 10 Mbps connections

The networking kits that come with cards you install in your computer will require you to have a PCI expansion slot available in your computer. These networking kits do not supply network cards for older, ISA expansion slots. You will also need to make sure you have at least 10 MB of hard disk space to install the networking software.

 Note: Currently available home phoneline networks operate with both PCs and Macintosh computers.

Parallel Port Connection

Installing the parallel connection is simple. Follow these short steps:

1. Unplug any printer that may be currently attached to your computers parallel port.
2. Plug in one end of the parallel cable to the network adapter.
3. Reattach the printer cable into the printer (normally an optional feature).
4. Attach the network adapter to the wall using a phone line.

USB Port Connection

It is not difficult to install the USB port network adapter. The main thing to remember is that the computer must be turned on when plugging the adapter into the computer for the first time. This will trigger the USB port installation.

Plug a phone cable between the USB adapter and the phone jack.

PCI Card Connection

When installing PCI cards, follow the installation instructions found in the Network Interface Cards section of this chapter. Installing and setting up this type of network card is really no different than the installation of a typical ethernet network card.

Once your network cards are installed, you are ready for software setup, covered in Chapter 5. The kits come with two network cards and more can be purchased. Unlike ethernet cards, home phoneline network cards are not compatible between brands. When purchasing additional cards, you must match the brands you have currently installed. One nice thing is that the new 10 Mbps cards are compatible with the slower, 1 Mbps cards on the same network.

General Connection Information

When installing computers on a phoneline network, each computer must be within 150 feet of the other computers being networked and close enough to a phone jack so that a normal telephone extension cable can be run.

Once the network adapter is installed in the computer, run the included phone cable adapter between the phone jack and the card, plugging it into the back of the card. For example, the Intel AnyPoint card marks this slot with the word "Wall." You can, at this point, also plug a telephone into the back of the card or adapter to continue using a phone from this location. Your phone will not interfere with the network data flowing over the phone line.

If you are networking two PCs in the same room, and there is only a single phone jack, it is perfectly fine to use a phone-line splitter found at any Radio Shack or electronics store. Splitters are available to split a single phone jack into one or many phone jacks. Purchase a splitter that allows you to network as many PCs as you need. The other option, if you are only networking two PCs and they are in the same room, is to forget the phone jack and just plug the cable between the two PCs, plugging the cable into the same jack you would have connected to the wall.

The following are some important things to keep in mind:

- If you are using noise filters or surge suppressors on your phone lines, you must unplug them and plug the home phone-line adapter cable directly into the phone jack.

- In homes with more than one telephone number, all of the PCs must be plugged into phone jacks with the same telephone number. It does not have to be a working telephone line—dial tone is not necessary. It is only necessary that the wires be connected physically with other jacks in the house where you wish to have computers on the network.

Setting Up Wireless LANS

When it comes to installation, there are no networking technologies simpler than wireless networking products. There is no cable required. This is certainly an added bonus if your home is difficult to wire, or you are renting and do not want to punch holes in the wall or ceiling to run cable. It is also the most adaptable, allowing you to move the location of your computer without worrying about the network connection. In some cases, you can even move your PC outside to enjoy the outdoors while you work.

As we discussed in Chapter 2, there are competing wireless technologies, primarily HomeRF and Wi-Fi (IEEE 802.11b). Because they operate in the same frequency range, there are installation issues common to both technologies—primarily, the need to get rid of the competing home appliances that operate in the same frequency range. Chapter 4 will discuss placement of radio equipment throughout your home in greater detail.

Whichever type of wireless technology you choose, you will need to place a wireless gateway, which converts wired network traffic into radio signals, at an optimal point in your home. If you are connecting your network to the Internet, you may consider a wireless DSL modem, like the one offered by Cayman Systems (*www.cayman.com*). Their ADSL modem works with both HomeRF and Wi-Fi networks.

HomeRF

HomeRF is not the fastest network in the world at 1.6 MB per channel, but it sure is easy to install. You can have at least ten devices operating on the network at one time, which is more than enough for most homes today. There are products that claim you can have up to 127 devices on the network, but with slow bandwidth be wary of those claims.

Each network device can be up to 150 feet from the wireless gateway, sometimes known as the connection point or bridge. The frequency-hopping spread spectrum transmitter/receiver units operate in the microwave range and should be immune to interference from even your home microwave oven. That does not mean you should put a transmitter directly next to it, however.

The most important thing you can do to have a successful HomeRF network is to perform a survey of your home. The radio devices used in HomeRF operate at the 2.4 GHz band. There are more devices, other than your microwave oven, that operate at this frequency. Some of the newer cordless phones operate at this frequency as well. If you intend to use any of these devices, you may experience trouble with your network.

Operating at low power, HomeRF is considered a PAN and not meant for networking large buildings, including large homes. The 150 foot distance is a maximum, and depending on the construction of your home, such as solid brick walls or concrete walls, this distance can be considerably less. You may have to move devices around to find the optimal radio reception.

Wi-Fi

Another wireless technology that is operating in the unlicensed microwave 2.4 and 5 GHz band is Wi-Fi or IEEE 802.11b and 802.11a. Offering much greater speeds than products like HomeRF, Wi-Fi comes in at a blazing 11 and 54 Mbps. This wireless technology has slowly emerged as the standard for wireless networking products. Another advantage of this technology is that you can operate PCs at ranges of 300 to 500 feet when using the slower 802.11b— quite a bit further than with HomeRF. The placement of the wireless access points and computers within the home is not as big of an issue with this technology.

One important consideration when finding a place for your equipment is the possible interference by other 2.4 GHz devices in the home. Position your equipment well away from microwave ovens and newer cordless phones and you should have no trouble. Microwaves tend to be noisier than telephones because they are not designed to operate within a narrow bandwidth of frequencies. In fact, if you have a wireless television repeater in the house to extend the reach of the cable or satellite TV system, you will quickly learn that microwaves send out a lot of noise. You will never stand next to one again while it is cooking dinner once you see how far the microwave radiation can travel through the house.

When installing a Wi-Fi wireless network, you will need to find a suitable place for the access point (bridge to your network hub). This is the one part of a wireless network that is not necessarily wireless. You will need to run a cat 5 cable between your network hub and the access point. One positive feature is that you will not necessarily need an ac outlet close to your access point when you use Power over Ethernet.

Power Over Ethernet

There are new innovations that have made wireless even more wireless. No system is completely wireless. You must run cat 5 cable from your hub to the access point, and then be able to provide power to the access point. This last point can be a major inconvenience if you do not happen to have a plug where the access point is best situated. Rather than install a new plug, or worse yet, run an extension cord, you should consider equipment that supports Power over Ethernet (PoE).

The power to drive the access point is sent through the cat 5 cable—the same one that connects the access point to your network hub. You simply provide the power using a small PoE module (injector) that uses the unused wires of a cat 5 cable to send power to your access point or remote PoE-compliant hardware.

You can also use PoE on devices that were not designed for PoE by using a special device called a tap. The tap acts like a splitter and routes the electricity sent over the cat 5 cable to the normal dc input of the device.

There are two types of PoE injectors:

• Passive

• Fault protected

Passive devices send dc voltage through the cat 5 cable with no protection. The amount of voltage sent across the cable can vary depending on the manufacturer of the equipment. The IEEE has set 48 VDC as the standard. The fault-protected injector provides short-circuit and over-voltage protection. Just as there are two types of injectors, there are also two types of taps:

• Passive

• Regulated

A passive tap simply accepts the dc voltage sent by the injector. What goes in comes out. A regulated tap allows you to convert the input voltage to a range of output voltages. These can range from 5 VDC to 12 VDC.

The single-port injector is probably sufficient for most home network applications. Multiport injectors are also available for situations in which you may need to power multiple remote devices.

Summary

Setting up your network hardware is the step you must take with the greatest amount of care. Proper hardware setup can mean the difference between a network that operates trouble free and one that causes you continual and difficult-to-find problems.

You will find that setting up your network with manufactured cables when possible will ease your network setup. When this is not possible, careful cable assembly is key to a successful network setup. Be careful not to exceed any of the distance limits.

Wireless networks are simpler to set up than wired networks but more susceptible to problems such as electronic interference. Careful selection of the transceiver position can help you increase the efficiency of your network. Chapter 4 will assist you in the task of running cable and selecting transceiver positions.

Setting up a
Home Network

4

Chapters 2 and 3 helped you select the type of network to install, and described the types of equipment and cables you will need to install the network. This chapter covers the actual installation of the network hardware. On the surface, this may seem like a simple task. There is definitely a right way and a wrong way to install your network hardware. This chapter will teach you about some of the tools you should have and will give some tips for correct installation.

In addition to showing you how to physically tie your computers together, we also explain the importance of documenting your network so that changing it in the future and troubleshooting problems becomes an easier task. Together, proper installation and good documentation will help you avoid messes such as the one shown in Figure 4.1.

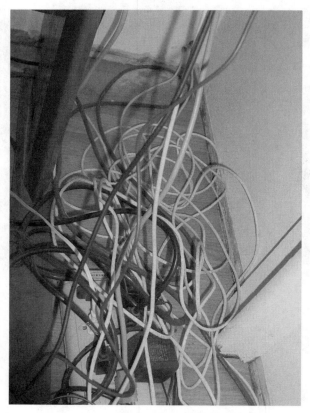

Figure 4.1 *For virtually pennies you can avoid this kind of mess.*

Planning the Network Layout

Correctly and efficiently planning your network can save you headaches and a great deal of time. Planning a wired network involves organizing the cable path for efficiency of network operation as well as aesthetics. On the other hand, planning a wireless network involves directing radio frequency around your home for maximum signal strength. Even though the physical labor expended during installation of a wireless network is quite a bit less, planning the network layout can be more challenging.

Tip: Take your time in the planning phase. There are all types of network configurations, and finding the one that works best for you now might not allow you to expand your network later.

Create a layout drawing. One of the easiest ways to visualize a network path is on paper. Draw a simple floor plan of your home. It is best if you use a computer drawing tool so you can make multiple copies of the floor plan. This will allow you to create several possible plans.

Planning a Wired Network

The primary consideration when planning a wired network is the location of existing and/or future computer equipment. Remember that new network devices are being created every day, so try to plan ahead. For example, it is conceivable that your refrigerator, telephone, and television may end up being connected to the Internet. Another device for which to plan ahead is your home-security system.

Once you have an idea of where your network-ready equipment should be located, you will need to know where network devices like hubs, routers, and modems will be placed. This brings us to a discussion of what is known in the networking world as *topology*. Topology is simply how the wires connect the different devices on a network.

There are three basic network topologies:

- **Star topology** – This is the basic configuration of most ethernet networks. It requires a hub.

- **Daisy chain** – Computer are connected one to another. This topology is rarely used and when it is, it is used in very inexpensive networks.

- **Ring** – The ring topology, also known as token ring, is shaped as it sounds. The network is designed to send information around the network in circles. A special token, or electronic permission slip, is passed around the network. When a computer in the ring receives a token, it then has permission to send data. The token reduces the amount of network traffic that collides with other network traffic. This topology is now rarely used.

The star topology, with a network hub at its center, is the most common way to connect computers in a network. This replaced the more widely used daisy-chain topology because of an inherent weakness in the daisy-chain design—the "Christmas light problem." When one computer in the chain fails, all other computers after the break do not receive a network signal.

When you have two computers in the same room and the hub is in another room, you can use a hub in the computers' room, enabling you to run only a single network cable into each room. Figure 4.2 shows an example of a poorly configured network, while Figure 4.3 is an example of one of the best ways to connect your home network.

Planning a Wireless Network

The suggestion to create a floor plan drawing of your house is even more important for wireless networks. You should note the type of each wall, such as brick, stone, wall board, etc., and if there is a fireplace. Radio signals will propagate (travel) through some types of walls and floors but not through others.

With a good plan, you will be able to get pretty close to the final configuration on paper. Unlike with wired networks, however you should plan to be a bit more flexible in your network design. If you use a cell phone, you know that even the best Radio Frequency (RF) engineers have a tough time achieving perfect radio coverage. You may end up having to move your equipment slightly to obtain the best results.

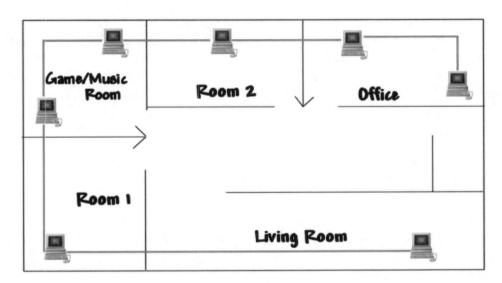

Figure 4.2 *This is a poor example of how to configure a network.*

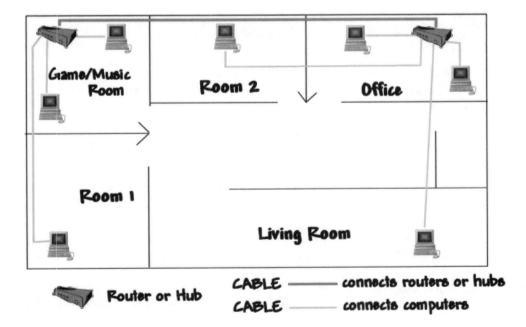

Figure 4.3 *This is one of the better examples of home-network configuration.*

Remember, in a wireless network you are trying to achieve maximum signal strength between the wireless hub and individual computers. The access-point hardware will send and receive signals to the computers on the network. When planning a location for your access point, you should find a place that is as central to each of the computers on the network as possible, and as high up as possible to avoid interference from doors, people, book cases, or other tall obstructions.

Note: It is not a good idea to place your access point hardware directly next to a ceiling fan, or in a position where the network signal will have to pass through a ceiling fan.

Some access-point hardware has an optional range-extender antenna. If your network is going to extend near the specified limits of your network hardware, you might consider obtaining a range-extender antenna if it is available from your network equipment vendor.

Network Cable

Network cable is typically eight-strand twisted pair. The diameter of the cable is narrow, around 3/16 of an inch, and comes in a variety of colors. Cables surrounded by a white jacket are preferable—they are hidden more easily along white walls. The neutral color also helps it blend well with other light colors. If your walls are a darker color, you might consider darker colored cable, painting over the cable, or running the cable where it cannot be seen.

The trick to cable installation is patience. There is nothing fun about running cable, but a job well done will work for a long time and it will not appear as though you thumbtacked the cable to the wall without care.

If you have ever run ac wire, phone wire, or cable TV wire through your home, then you have already mastered the hard part of running Unshielded Twisted Pair (UTP) cable. The key in the process is planning. Know where the cables should run and how long they need to be. Use the information in the following sections and you should have no trouble at all.

Tip: While remodeling or building a home, you should instruct the electrical contractors to install cat 5 cable and RJ45 wall jacks to save you time and effort later.

Hidden Installation

When building or remodeling a house, and before the wall covering is installed, it makes sense to install network cable. Talk to your electrical contractor. Most electrical contractors are becoming familiar with the installation of network cable and even fiber optics in new homes. Many new homes are advertised as network-ready by the builder.

Many of us are not fortunate enough to be installing a network into a brand new home—instead, most of us retrofit our existing homes with network cable. Hiding the network cable will add to the value and maintain the beauty of your home. Network cable can be run through the attic, down through the walls, through crawl spaces and basements, and even through air conditioning conduit. It definitely takes more work to conceal the cable, but it is worth the extra work to keep your home beautiful.

There is one potential downside to hiding your network cable in the walls. It is possible that years in the future, network technology will change and cat 5 wire may no longer remain the standard cable. You would then have to run new network cable—perhaps even fiber optic cable. However, it is unlikely that hiding cat 5 cables will present a problem. Advances in network technology, such as gigabit ethernet, use cat 5 wire.

What You Will Need

Using the right tool for the right job will not only make the job simpler, it will make it possible. Running network cable through walls is particularly challenging without the right tools. The following is a list of the essential tools:

- Drill motor
- Long-spade drill bit, wider than the cable
- Fish tape (Figure 4.4)
- Tape measure
- Marker
- Staple gun

- U-shaped staples (Figure 4.10)
- Small keyhole saw or electric jigsaw
- Crimp tool and RJ45 connectors

Working from the plan drawing we suggested you create earlier in this chapter, you should decide how you will run your network cable through the house. If working from an attic, it is best to start in the attic since it is easiest to drop network cable down through the wall. If working from the basement, you might find it easiest to begin in the basement and push the wire up into the wall. Most of the time, the place from which your network cable exits the wall will be close to the floor, so the distance you have to push the network cable up is fairly short.

Tip: Do not terminate the ends of the network cable until you have finished running all of the cable.

When working from the attic, you will probably have to move insulation out of the way to reveal the top of the wall. You will notice that it is capped by a two by four. The upright supports (studs) of your house are also likely to be two by fours placed approximately 16 inches apart. You should be able to see where the nails are set down into these studs. If this wall is a bearing wall—one that supports the weight of the roof—it may have a double two by four cap. You will know that it is a bearing wall because there will be studs holding the roof up. It is easiest to avoid running cable through a bearing wall, though it is not impossible to run cable through one.

Figure 4.4 *Use a fish tape to pull network cable through walls and conduit.*

In the room in which you want the network connection to exit the wall, you should cut a small hole where you would like the network cable to exit. For best results, you can purchase a box similar to that in which your ac power plugs are mounted and mount that inside the wall. This will make it simple to install a faceplate to cover your hole in the wall or install a female RJ45 connector. There are faceplates available with a small round hole, like the type used for older telephones before RJ11 modular connectors were used. You may also purchase solid faceplates and drill a hole for the cable to pass through.

In the attic or basement, drill a hole through the cap in the wall or base of the wall (respectively) using the long-spade drill bit and drill motor. Then pass the network cable through the wall. If you have difficulty passing the cable through the wall, use the fish tape to pull the cable through. Make sure you pull enough cable through the wall to reach the computer or hub. It is always a good idea to pull more than you need.

Whether you are in the attic or basement, run the network cable along the path of the wall. Fasten the cable to the wall every few feet using a staple gun. Of course, be careful not to drive the staple through the cable. Run the cable along the wall, even in the attic, so that while moving around in the attic you will not accidentally snag and rip the network cable.

Tip: If you accidentally drive a staple through the network cable, you can assume that the cable is damaged at that point. You can salvage the cable by cutting it, and installing a female and male jack, reconnecting the cable.

It is a good idea to label the cable in the attic or basement, especially since it is so much harder to know where the wires are going in dark areas. After running each network cable, label the hub end of the cable. When you have finished running the cable, follow the directions in Chapter 3 for installing the connectors on the end of the cable.

Each port in the hub or router has a number. On the computer end of the cable, you can label the cable with the number of the port into which the other end is plugged. That will make troubleshooting much easier than if you had to unplug cables to see which lights on the hub go out, especially if the lights are already out because of a problem.

Making the Job Easier

Installing the network cables into the walls is aesthetically pleasing but quite difficult and more expensive. Most people opt to run the network cable along the exterior of the wall. You can move the network cable from room to room by drilling a small hole in the wall and passing the cable through it. Because you will want to run as few cables as possible, use more than one hub throughout the house if networking more than two computers.

The most important part of a successful network cabling job is using the right tools and hardware. For this reason we will cover tools in some detail before describing the steps you need to take to install the cable.

Drills

Having the right drill can mean getting the job done quickly and easily or not at all. Having a drill bit that can reach all the way through walls is essential. Figure 4.5 shows a couple examples of drills still in their packaging.

There are long drills specially made for running wire through walls. They are commonly used by telephone repairmen, and you can find them at larger hardware stores. These special bits have a small hole drilled in them as shown in Figure 4.6, to help guide cable and wire through walls.

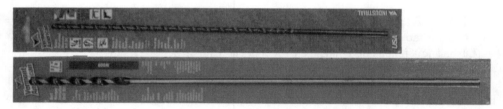

Figure 4.5 *Long-spade drills.*

Figure 4.6 *Some drill bits used by telephone installers have a hole drilled in them.*

Fasteners

Take a look at Figure 4.1. There is a way to avoid that kind of a mess, and that is by using plastic tie wraps (Figure 4.7 and Figure 4.8). They can be purchased at any hardware store. When you are running multiple network cables to your hub, it is a good idea to tie them together into a bundle. Also, if the network cable you have running out of the wall is not stapled, you might consider tie-wrapping it to stationary devices to keep people from tripping over it or having it become inadvertently cut or torn.

There are many types of tie wraps. One convenient type of tie wrap is the ID tag variety (Figure 4.9). Using a permanent marker, you can write on the plastic ID tags and tie wrap them right on the cable. This makes them easy to read and ensures that the label will not be inadvertently torn from the cable.

Another type of tie wrap comes with a release mechanism. Most inexpensive tie wraps, once cinched, will not release. The advantage of using a tie wrap with a release mechanism is twofold. First, you can easily tie and untie a bundle of cables. Second, it is very easy to accidentally cut a cable while trying to cut a tie wrap.

Staples

When installing network cable, it is common to use a staple gun. Staple guns are available almost everywhere. When shopping for a staple gun for cable installation, you might want to select the staple before selecting the staple gun. There is a right and wrong type of staple to use in this application. Figure 4.10 shows photos of both the correct (U-shaped) staple, and the incorrect (box-shaped) staple. The U-shaped staple will hold the network cable without compressing it—compressing it may damage the wires within the cable.

Figure 4.7 *Fasten multiple cables with tie wraps.*

Figure 4.8 *Plastic tie wraps can help organize your network cables.*

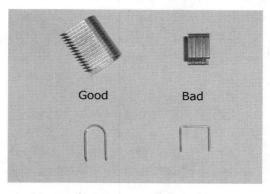

Figure 4.9 *ID tag tie wraps can save you a great deal of time and frustration when troubleshooting a network.*

Figure 4.10 *It is important to use the correct type of staple.*

Once you have located the correct, U-shaped staples, read the box to find out which type of staple gun will accept these staples, and then purchase that type of gun. This type of staple is also handy for other household purposes, such as putting up holiday lights. The curved shape will keep from damaging the electric cable running to the lights.

Installing the Cable

No matter how you choose to run your network cable—in the walls, through the ceiling, under the floor, or strung through the air—there are some basic do's and don'ts (see Table 4.1).

Table 4-1 Cabling Do's and Dont's

Tip	Explanation
Do avoid running cable under furniture.	Running network wiring under furniture may eventually lead to having the leg of a piece of furniture crush the cable. The cable may be pulled and broken when furniture is moved.
Do use less than ten pounds of tension on the network cable.	Pulling long lengths of network cable can pull the tiny wires inside the cable apart. Use two people—one to feed cable, and one to pull. Do not stretch the cable tight against the wall.
Don't bend the cables.	When pulling the cable, or passing the cable through walls and floors, it is important not to bend the cable. When pulling the cable through conduit with 90 degree bends, use special pulling ends that have a removable cover plate.
Don't run cable under rugs.	Running a cable under a rug will cause mechanical stress on the network cable, eventually causing it to break. It will also cause a wear spot in your rug. If you must run the cable under a rug, use special wiring protectors made for this purpose.
Don't run the cable where a pet can get to it.	Pets love to chew, and there seems to be something particularly yummy about network cable. When fastened to a wall, network cable is harder for pets to access.

Table 4-1 Cabling Do's and Don'ts *(continued)*

Tip	Explanation
Don't kink the cable in corners.	It is always tempting to make the sharpest corner possible when running a network cable around a corner. There should always be an arc in the cable at least the size of a normal drinking glass so that wires are not twisted and broken.
Don't squeeze too hard with the tie wraps.	When fastening cables together or to a fastening device, do not cinch the cable tie too hard. It can sever the small wires inside the cable.
Don't pinch the cables with staples.	Be careful when using a staple gun. It is very easy to drive a staple through the cable, cutting or shorting wires inside the cable.
Don't allow the cables to touch any hot surface.	Even though most cables have fire-retardant jackets, it is important not to run the cable next to hot things such as radiators, heaters, flourescent light fixtures, or other light fixtures.
Don't run network cable too close to the power cable.	Power cables radiate noise. Running a network cable next to an ac power cable can cause interference on the network cable. Try to keep the network cable at least six inches from a power cable and never run them through the same conduit.

Following your plan, begin running the network cable from the hub. It is easiest to run the cable along the top of the baseboard running along the bottom of the wall. If the wall is hard plaster, it will be easiest to staple the cable into the baseboard. Trying to staple into a hard plaster or brick wall is not only dangerous, but will probably damage your network cable.

When you are ready to put the network cable through the wall, use the long-spade drill, normally 12 to 18 inches long, to drill through the wall. Drill from the room you want the network cable to enter, not the one where it already is. Drill the hole, then STOP! Do not pull the drill out of the hole once it has been drilled. Leave the drill poking through the wall. This is very important. Go into the room where the pointy end of the drill should be poking through the wall. There are several things you can do at this point.

Many drills of this type have a small hole in the end of the drill where a wire or strong braided string (like dental floss) can be tied. If your drill has this type of hole (recommended), tie a wire or string through this hole and then tape the other end of the string or wire to the end of the network cable. It is best to use two people for this next step. While one person pulls the drill back out of the wall, the other should carefully feed the network cable into the hole. Once the drill is out of the hole, the string or wire can be used to continue pulling the network cable the rest of the way through the wall.

If your drill does not have a hole like the one we described, it is possible to tape the network cable to the end of the drill using a strong tape such as electrical tape. Normal scotch tape is not strong enough and may break when pulled.

What if you have drilled the hole and pulled the drill out, or were not successful at feeding the network cable through the wall? Use the fish tape to help guide the network cable through the wall. Feed the fish tape from the room where you drilled the hole, and pull the network cable through the hole carefully. Remember to not put much pressure on the cable by stretching it or pulling it hard.

The following are a few more installation tips:

- Avoid drilling within a few inches of the room corners. If you drill too close to the corners you will find two by fours and you do not want to drill through them.

- Make sure you are not drilling into other wires or pipes. Drilling into an electric ac wire is very dangerous.

- Avoid installing wiring in damp or wet areas such as bathrooms, along basement floors, and outside walls. Some government regulations require that telephone jacks in bathrooms be a minimum of four meters (about 13 feet) away from a bathing area.

Staples are used to keep the cable close to the wall. The cable should be stapled every three feet. Remember that the staples will keep the cable from sliding to either side, so make sure you have enough cable on both ends before stapling. Plan ahead. It will be difficult to remove all of the staples just to slide the cable.

Cable Distance

The distance that a network can run, from the point where a signal originates to the last computer or device connected to the network, is 100 meters (around 330 feet). The reason for this limit is to eliminate data loss and data transmission errors. The signal strength diminishes as it travels along the network cable. Distances greater than 100 meters without any boosting of the signal will begin to cause data loss and transmission errors. Hubs will let you increase that distance by an additional 100 meters. To achieve this result, you will need a FastHub (most hubs are FastHubs). Refer to Figures 4.11 and 4.12 for examples of network configurations showing the distance limits.

Installation Tips

Running network cable seems like a simple job, that can be done well by anyone with a free half hour and a staple gun. Do not let the job deceive you. The following sections include a few helpful hints that you should heed before taking on this task.

Take Your Time

Do not rush the job. There is nothing more aggravating than to spend time running network cable, perhaps even through the walls of your home, to find out later that in a hurry to get finished, you have torn a cable, broken a wire, or run a staple through the network cable jacket.

Figure 4.11 *The distance between the hub and computer is a maximum of 100 meters.*

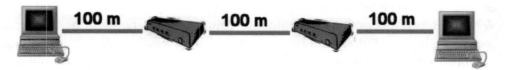

Figure 4.12 *Adding an additional FastHub will give you 100 meters more.*

Do Not Underestimate the Job

As in the previous recommendation, make sure you give yourself enough time to do the job. Be liberal when purchasing the accessories you need to install the network hardware. It may take several attempts to correctly terminate a network cable. Purchase plenty of extra RJ45 connectors. Buy plenty of cable, not the exact amount. It is important that the network cable be relaxed and not just stretched or bent sharply. The worst consequence of poor planning is to run cable through walls, floors, and ceilings and then find you have not allowed enough cable to reach the destination.

Try Not To Do It By Yourself

It is a good idea to work with a partner when installing a network. Pulling cable is almost impossible to do well by yourself. Without someone on one end to feed the cable, it is possible to nick the cable or break wires. Another even more important reason to work with someone else is the risk involved when working at heights. It is never a good idea to work on a ladder alone. Besides, the job will be faster and easier if you have help.

Use More Than One Hub

When designing your network, it is a good idea (if you can afford it) to plan for more than one hub throughout the house. This will enable you to expand your network easily in the future.

Label the Cables

Perhaps the single most important installation tip is to label all of the cables on both ends. It does not matter if you use scotch tape, paper tape, or more expensive ID tag tie wrap labels. Trying to figure out later where each wire should go can be time consuming and unnecessary.

Simple and Cheap Solutions

When running network cable outdoors you can get as fancy or as simple as you like. The simplest solution is to run a long network cable outside where you need a network connection. Most network cable is moisture proof, but not sun proof, so it is best to bury cable or protect it from the sun when possible.

If you are going to leave your network cable outside, in a place where it is not protected from weather, we recommend placing a plastic bag over the cable end when not in use. Seal it with a rubber band or some other fastener. This will help keep moisture away from the end of the cable. Moisture will cause the cable pins to corrode, not allowing for a good network connection—or worse, damaging your network card.

Tip: If you bury your cable, mark its location so that you do not inadvertently cut the cable when digging.

Fancy but Better Solutions

When leaving a network connection outside, it is a better idea to run the network cable in some type of weatherproof conduit. This conduit can be made of either metal or plastic. The following are some reasons you might consider when deciding whether or not to spend the money for conduit:

- Protects the cable from the elements
- Protects the cable from rodents, such as gophers, rabbits, rats and mice
- Protects the cable from inadvertent cutting during digging
- Allows you to run the cable above ground, protecting it from moisture and the sun

When running your cable in conduit, we do not recommend putting a male connector on the outdoor end. Instead, there are waterproof junction boxes normally used for outdoor electric connections. Install a female connector on the end of the cable, in the waterproof junction box. This is important. The cable *must* be wired as a crossover cable when terminating it with a female connector. That way, in order to use the outdoor connection, you simply have to use a normal short whip (network cable) to connect to the female connector.

People with home offices are finding that they enjoy working outdoors. If you are interested in using your computer outside, you might also consider a wireless network in addition to your wired LAN. This next section discusses setting up wireless network hardware.

Phoneline and Powerline Networks

Phoneline and powerline networks are similar when it comes to setting up network equipment. Both of these networks take advantage of the wires already in your walls, rather than installing new cable. One of the big advantages over running new cable is that you normally have multiple electric plugs in each room, and most homes have several telephone jacks already installed.

Phoneline and Powerline networks are the easiest and fastest to connect, compared to other home networks. Basically you just have to plug a wire from your computer's specialized network card into the wall and install the software (covered in the Chapter 5). Most software automatically detects the computer and devices on the network.

Equipment Placement

Place your computer conveniently next to either a phone jack or electric outlet, depending on the type of network you are using. Regardless of the type of network, your computer is connected to it using an NIC, USB port, or parallel port. Figure 4.13 and Figure 4.14 show examples of how these networks are connected.

The connections for the powerline network will vary depending on which product you have purchased. For example, if you have the Intellon network, your computer is connected to the network by connecting the Intellon NIC directly to any ac power outlet. (see Figure 4.15). The Intelogis adapter connects your computer to the network using a parallel cable. The parallel cable connects between the power outlet on the wall and your computer's parallel port. The Initial Power Packet (IPP) uses an adapter that connects to the power outlet and from there, depending on the model, to your computer using a USB cable or ethernet cable. Figure 4.16 shows an example of this connection.

PCI Phoneline Card

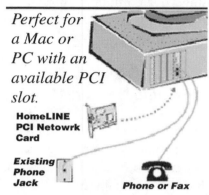

Perfect for a Mac or PC with an available PCI slot.

HomeLINE PCI Netowrk Card

Existing Phone Jack

Phone or Fax

Figure 4.13 *Connections are made from the jack on the wall to the computer's network card to the telephone.*

USB-to-Phoneline Adapter

Perfect for a USB-equipped Mac or PC

HomeLINE USB to Phoneline Adapter

Existing Phone Jack

Phone or Fax

Figure 4.14 *Connections are made from the jack on the wall to the USB adapter to the computer's USB port and the telephone.*

Testing the Line Noise

The time it takes for data on a network to move from one place on the network to another is dependent on many different things. Here are some of the physical limits to network speed:

- Depending on the brand of network you are using, a phoneline network allows data to travel at different speeds, the maximum being 10 Mpbs.
- Powerline networks have a maximum speed of 14 Mpbs. You can only reach this speed if you are using an NIC.
- The maximum speed for USB ports is 2 Mbps.
- The maximum speed for parallel ports is 360 Kbps.
- The maximum speed for serial ports is 115 Kbps.

Figure 4.15 *The computer NIC connects directly to the power outlet. This is an Intellum card.*

Figure 4.16 *The adapter is connected to the wall and from there it can be connected via a parallel, USB, or Ethernet port. This an Initial parallel adapter.*

Considering that the fastest connection of a dial-up modem is only 56 Kbps, each of these networks is still faster and will give you good results.

Line noise, whether on the phone line or on the power line, can cause the network to fail when sending packets of data, causing the network to retry. Most networks today are fault tolerant, meaning that the network tries to correct each of its errors. The downside to this fault tolerance is efficiency. It takes time for the network to resend missing packets of data across the network. The more the network fails to deliver packets, or fails to deliver a valid packet, the more it has to retry, causing network traffic to run slower.

The amount of time a computer waits for a response from a network is called *latency*. On an ethernet-based network, the latency is about 1 ms (millisecond). On telephone lines you might be able to get the same latency as an ethernet-based network, but most of the time the latency could range from 20 ms to 50 ms. The powerline network has the worst latency of all—it can vary from 40 ms to 400 ms and is determined largely by the quality of the ac power cables.

The only good way to test the line for noise or speed is to connect the network. If you have a PC, you can use the MS-DOS command prompt to send a test signal, called a ping, to other computers on the network. For Macs, there is a program called IPNet Monitor from Sustainable Softworks. IPNet Monitor will help you detect problems with your network. The ping program sends several test messages to another computer's address and reports how long it took the message to receive a response. If you are experiencing high latency, you know you have a noise problem on your network. If you receive no result from a ping, you have more serious problems. Chapter 9 covers Ping and other network testing utilities in greater detail.

Splitters

If you are setting up more than one computer in a single room and you have a limited number of places to plug in your network, it is possible to expand both phoneline and powerline networks.

Expand the phoneline network by using a telephone extension plug or multi-line jack, also known as a splitter (Figure 4.17). You can get extensions that have two to five additional plugs.

Extend a powerline network by using an extension cord or any multi-plug device (Figure 4.18). You have to consider that by expanding the distance of the network, you might increase the noise level on the line and consequently achieve poor data transfer rates. Some powerline network adapters might have a problem with some extension plugs—be sure to read the hardware manual to make sure you are using the correct plugs.

When plugging a phoneline network into the only phone jack in the room, you have monopolized the only phone jack in the room. Most phoneline networks have extension jacks that allow you to connect a modem or telephone. In the event that it does not, you will need to use one of the multiport phone jacks to increase the number of phone jacks in the room.

 Note: Some powerline networks will not work if plugged into surge protectors.

Power Supplies and Filters

Keeping your network running with today's unreliable power supply can be an important issue. No matter how good you are backing up and saving your work on a regular basis, no one can be completely ready for an unexpected blackout.

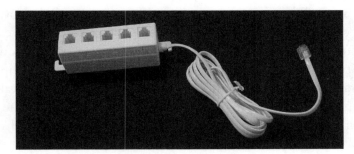

Figure 4.17 *Five-plug multiline extension*

Figure 4.18 *Read the hardware manual to determine if this type of extention will work properly.*

Uninterruptible Power Supplies

Electric power in the United States, once considered the most reliable of any place in the world, is no longer that reliable. Brownouts, rolling blackouts, and just plain power failures can cause computer systems to instantly lose power—or more devastating, lose power and then intermittently regain power.

Using an Uninterruptible Power Supply (UPS) can save you a great deal of money and aggravation. It consists of batteries with an inverter to change the dc electricity of the battery into ac electricity used by your computer hardware. You will find UPSs rated in amps. Many of the boxes will tell you how long they will power a typical computer system should the power fail. Most computer and office supply stores carry UPSs.

Some UPS systems come with a special cable that, when used with a compatible operating system, will gracefully shut down your computer. This is a great feature if you are not home. It can be a terrible feature if you are working at your computer and it unexpectedly shuts down before you have had a chance to save your work.

Surge Protectors

Something as simple as using surge protectors can ensure that your computer equipment continues to run for many years. Surge protectors are most often used as multi-plug extension cords more than anything else. A good surge protector can protect your expensive computer and network equipment from harmful surges in current from the ac voltage coming from the wall.

Power surges can come from many different sources. One of the most well-known sources of electric power surges is lightening. In midwestern and southern states this can be quite a problem.

 Warning! Simply plugging your electronic equipment into a surge protector is not a guarantee against damage during an electrical storm. It is strongly suggested that you shut down all computers and nonessential electronic equipment during such a storm and unplug the equipment from the wall.

Harmonic Distortion Filters

Harmonic distortion is a type of noise created by power supplies for electronic appliances such as computers, televisions, stereos, and other digital electronics.

The noise is created when these power supplies take the ac sine wave that comes out of the wall, and converts it to a square wave. The noise from this conversion is fed back out onto the electric grid. In small, isolated areas, such as the island of Oahu in Hawaii, this harmonic distortion can cause electric and electronic equipment to burn up even while turned off. Many people are plagued by harmonic distortion and cannot figure out why they go through one computer after another or must replace stereo equipment on a regular basis. There are special filtering devices available if you are experiencing this type of problem in your neighborhood.

Tip: If you experience equipment failure, note the time and date of the failure and contact your local power company to see if they had a harmonic distortion "event." If so, some power companies will replace your equipment free of charge.

If you are concerned about your sensitive electronics, you might consider balancing your ac power using a balanced power isolation transformer. They tend to be on the expensive side, but could possibly save you many thousands of dollars in equipment. For more information, visit the Furman Sound Web site (*http://www.furmansound.com/BalPwr.html*). Audio enthusiasts have been using this type of equipment to remove noise and hum from their equipment for many years.

Fiber Network Planning

Using copper wire is not the only way to wire a house. If you are thinking of installing wire in the wall, and expect it to be useful for many years, you might consider the installation of fiber optics. It is true that not many products interface directly with fiber today, but it is only a matter of time (and some say not a long time) before using copper is considered a thing of the past. Fiber optics use laser light to transmit data rather than electrical impulses over copper wire.

Fiber networks are

• Fast

• Impervious to electrical noise, lightning, and flooding

• Cost effective

The bandwidth limits of fiber optics far exceed those of wired and wireless networks. There are fiber networks today with multigigabit bandwidths. Compare multi-gigabit (billions of bits per second) connections to the fast broadband connections of 1.5 megabits (1.5 million bits per second)—the bandwidth limitations of fiber far exceed those of copper wire. In fact, the limits of a single strand of fiber are now approaching a bandwidth capacity of one terabit, or one trillion bits per second.

Fiber optics, once delicate glass strands, are now made of durable plastic. Developments in plastic fiber have helped drive down cost while making the development of community-wide fiber networks a reality. The one drawback to fiber is that it is currently more difficult to terminate a fiber connection than an electrical connection such as those described earlier in the chapter.

The following is a comparison of costs for the installation of several types of network services from an April 20, 2001 Business 2.0 magazine article:

- Hybrid fiber-coaxial cable (HFC) $1,907
- DSL $2,484
- Fiber $2,385

Darryl Ponder, of Optical Solutions, says of fiber optics cabling, "it's reliable, long-lasting, impervious to storms and lightning, and a future-proof investment."

Fiber optics have been used by phone companies to provide voice communication since the 1970s. It has only been in the last decade that bandwidth requirements have increased to support Internet connections. Fiber was the obvious choice to create data-heavy trunk lines that stretched across the globe.

This book has pointed out the distance limitations of both cat 5 wire and wireless connections. After planning a network within those limitations, it will astound you to learn that the signal distance limitation of a fiber strand can exceed 100 kilometers.

Wireless Networks

One of the major advantages of a wireless network is the fact that there are few or no wires to run. There are three tasks involved in setting up a wireless network. The first is installing the wireless network cards in your computer. The second is setting up the wireless access point, and the third is testing for signal strength.

Installing Wireless Network Cards

Detailed information on installation of an NIC can be found in Chapter 2. Your wireless network card, when used with an access point (discussed in the next section) must match channel configurations with the access-point hardware. Some access points are designed to scan all possible channels, while others must be configured manually. You will need to refer to the user guide that comes with your equipment to see if you need to set the channel and how to do it.

Install your network card in a free PCI or ISA slot, depending on the type of network card you have purchased. If you have purchased a USB wireless network card, you should connect it to one of your USB ports. Once the card is installed in your computer, and before you turn the computer back on, you will most likely need to attach an external antenna.

Locate the newly installed NIC on the back of your computer. If your wireless network card requires the use of an external antenna, locate the connection for the antenna and carefully attach it.

Warning! When moving your computer into its final resting position, you must take extra caution not to damage the antenna.

Once your NIC is installed, you can return your computer to its normal resting place. Computers with wireless network cards will operate more efficiently if the computer is not enclosed within a computer desk cabinet. If you have difficulty establishing a good signal, you may need to move your computer to various positions around your workspace.

Wireless networks can communicate peer-to-peer (sometimes known as ad-hoc mode) or communicate to a central location that bridges your wireless network devices to a wired network. Operating in peer-to-peer mode, the computers will communicate directly with each other's wireless network cards. In this case, you must carefully position each computer for optimal radio communication. The disadvantage of operating in this mode is that the antenna is positioned very low to the ground because that is where computers are normally positioned. That would make everything from your chair to the pet cat barriers to signal propagation.

Access-Point Installation

Access points are used when connecting your wireless network to an existing wired network. For those of you who are connecting to the Internet using a cable modem or DSL modem, you will need to create a wired network to connect your modem to an access point. This acts as a wireless bridge to your network. Placement of the wireless access point (network transceiver) is one of the most important considerations when installing a wireless network. There are several types of access points, distinguished by where they are mounted. There are wall-mountable and ceiling-mountable devices.

When planning where your access-point hardware will be mounted, your most important consideration will be the availability of an ac outlet. When installing a ceiling-mountable access point, you may consider also installing an ac plug in the ceiling next to the access-point hardware.

Note: It is always best to have your home's electrical outlets installed by a licensed electrician.

In addition to having an ac outlet available when connecting your access point hardware to a cable modem or DSL modem, or connecting your wireless network to an existing wired network, you will need to run a network cable to your access point. For ceiling-mounted access points, follow the suggestions in Table 4.1 for running network cable through a ceiling.

Before permanently mounting your access point hardware to the wall or ceiling, it is a good idea to test your equipment to make certain that you will have adequate wireless signal strength. The next section discusses signal strength. Of course, if you are networking more than one computer in a single room, and the room has few large vertical obstructions, it is alright to mount the hardware permanently before testing.

Some access-point hardware requires the installation of a PC card interface. If your access-point equipment requires a PC (PCMCIA) card, insert it securely into the PC slot before mounting the hardware to the wall or ceiling.

Using the mounting hardware supplied with your access-point equipment, mount the hardware. It is recommended to have two people available when mounting equipment overhead or when using a ladder. The location of your access-point equipment should be free of moisture and dust. In other words, do not install it next to a bathroom door where steam from the shower may escape or under a window where dust and moisture may blow in. Most access-point hardware will also require adequate air flow so that the unit does not become overheated.

Signal Strength

Most wireless network hardware will test signal strength as a normal part of its diagnostics. This is a software tool you will run after installing the network software. Installing and configuring network software is covered in detail in Chapter 5. Once your software is set up, you will run the diagnostic tests to see if the signal strength is adequate for your network to operate.

Just like with a mobile phone, interference and dead spots can appear anywhere. If you are installing a Wi-Fi network, you will be happy to know that it maintains a network connection (without dropping your network connection). When the signal is weak, the connection speed is reduced before the network connection dies completely. If it does die, the signal comes right back when you move your equipment back within range.

Most of the diagnostics and signal strength testers are very rudimentary. Network installation professionals often have sophisticated and expensive tools to help you test your wireless LAN—the WildPacket AiroPeek software runs detailed diagnostics on wireless networks (*http://www.wildpackets.com/products/airopeek*).

Some home networks are used for home offices. Because wires are not required for connection to your local network, it is possible for a hacker to gain access to your network, possibly gaining access to sensitive business or personal financial information. Installation of software such as Airopeek not only charts signal strength, but can continuously scan for failed authentication attempts (network connection attempts). When the software discovers a possible security breach, it will capture traffic exchanged in these authentication attempts, making it possible to identify the potential attacker.

If your signal strength is insufficient or your network software reports a problem connecting to the network, try moving your equipment. If you try moving the equipment and you are still unable to connect, try moving your computer closer to the access-point hardware. Try testing the signal again. If your tests continue to fail, you may have installed the hardware incorrectly or the equipment may be failing. If the computer is able to connect to the network, try moving your computer further away from the access point. Do this until the signal is lost and you should be able to determine what is blocking the radio signal.

Summary

Installing a home network is not difficult. Remember to follow all of the safety rules with regard to working in high places and with electricity. Also, be patient. Installing the hardware correctly will save you headaches later on. If you need assistance, there are many commercial network installers available. You can find them in the phone book or online.

Configuring
Software 5

Installing a network involves both hardware and software setup. Once your network is physically installed, including the network cards and hubs or wireless repeaters, your next step is to install the software and configure the network settings. This chapter gives step-by-step instructions for configuring the network features of different operating systems to complete your home network setup.

Basic Information

Computers communicate with one another with a variety of predefined groups of commands, queries, and responses. These groups, like minilanguages, are known as *protocols*. There are several protocols involved when a computer begins communicating over a network. These protocols ensure that, no matter what type of computer is communicating or where it is located, it will understand the communication language of the other computers on the network. One of the most important of these protocols is called IP, or Internet Protocol.

Part of IP is the ability of computers to locate other computers on a network, whether they are sitting next to them, or on the other side of the world from them. This is done by giving each computer a unique numeric address called an IP address. A central registry, called the Internet Assigned Numbers Authority (IANA) is responsible for handing out these addresses to large organizations or companies, such as your Internet Service Provider (ISP). The ISP is then responsible for allocating these addresses to its customers' computers.

Static vs. Dynamic IP Addresses

There are two mechanisms that an ISP uses to hand out IP addresses. One mechanism is to give you an IP address to enter into your computer when you sign up with their service. This is known as a *static IP address* because while you use the particular ISP's service, this address will not change. The other mechanism is to allow its server computers to provide your computer an IP address dynamically each time your computer connects and logs in. This mechanism for retrieving a new IP address each time your computer connects employs another protocol known as Dynamic Host Control Protocol (DHCP).

Your Network IP Addresses

When planning your home network, you will have to plan how your computers will obtain IP addresses. Here are the options:

- Purchase multiple static IP addresses from your ISP.
- Assign local IP addresses and use a single ISP-assigned IP address, whether it be static or dynamically assigned, using DHCP.

Multiple ISP-Assigned IP Addresses

By far the easiest thing to do technically when planning your network is to secure an IP address for each computer on your network from your ISP. Unfortunately, this is also usually the most expensive option. Remember that ISPs are only allotted a certain number of IP addresses from IANA, so they are treated like gold, and that is exactly how you will have to pay for them. Expect the request for more than one IP address to be met with a smile and a call from the ISP's business unit.

If cost is not an obstacle, there are distinct advantages to giving each computer its own ISP-allotted IP address. Each computer will have an IP address that is known to other computers on the Internet. This makes communicating with other computers on the Internet simpler, and gives you access to more software programs that will not operate when your computer uses a local IP address.

Local IP Addresses

There are special IP number ranges for use in private or local area networks. These number ranges are reserved for use by any local area network. It is not possible for computers on the Internet to recognize these IP addresses.

RFC 1918 assigns the following IP address ranges to local networks (private internets).

10.0.0.0	– 10.255.255.255	(10 or 8 prefix)
172.16.0.0	– 172.31.255.255	(172.16 or 12 prefix)
192.168.0.0	– 192.168.255.255	(192.168 or 16 prefix)

Note: You can use IP addresses outside this range without coordination with IANA or your ISP, but these addresses must be used strictly on your local network, and not used on the public Internet.

The advantage to using these numbers is that it conserves the number of globally unique IP addresses. See Appendix A for a complete list of global IP address allocations.

The two most common number ranges are 10.x.x.x and 192.168.x.x. Give each computer in your network a number, starting with number 10. For example:

Computer A: 10

Computer B: 11

Computer C: 12

Computer D: 13

In this example, we are going to use the IP range 192.168.X.X. Each computer in the network will have an IP address as follows:

Computer A: 192.168.0.10

Computer B: 192.168.0.11

Computer C: 192.168.0.12

Computer D: 192.168.0.13

Static ISP-Assigned IP Addresses

Internet IP addresses are distributed by your ISP. Every computer that connects to the Internet must use an Internet IP address to send and receive traffic over the Internet. Because the number of IP addresses your ISP has been allotted by the Internet Assigned Numbers Authority (IANA), they limit the number of addresses assigned permanently (statically) to a customer. These addresses are normally distributed to business customers that run software that require the same IP addresses at all times. Home customers rarely require static IP addresses, and instead make use of dynamically assigned IP addresses using DHCP.

DHCP

A DHCP server manages a block of IP addresses. When a client computer such as the one you might use to connect to the Internet connects to your ISP, it will request a new IP address and install it on your computer until your connection is terminated.

There are advantages and disadvantages to DHCP. The advantage for the ISP is that it may have been assigned a thousand IP addresses by IANA. This would normally limit your ISP to only 1000 customers. The theory is that not everyone is logged in all the time. If a DHCP server manages that block of 1000 IP addresses, it hands them out on a first-come, first-served basis and reassigns them once customers begin to log out. This enables the ISP to have more customers. Theoretically, if 1000 customers logged in simultaneously, no other clients would be able to log in. This is a definite disadvantage when you happen to be customer number 1001.

Another disadvantage is that some software designed to communicate over a network requires that it know the IP address of a computer. When the IP address of the computer it is trying to contact changes, this becomes more difficult. Fewer software today relies on static IP addresses due to this disadvantage.

You will learn more about DHCP servers in Chapter 7. You can run your own DHCP server on your home network, allowing all of the computers on your network to connect to the Internet sharing a single Internet IP address while making use of special, non-Internet, local IP addresses.

The Mechanics of an IP Address

IP addresses are constructed of four groups of numbers separated by periods (dots). The structure of an IP address is also known as *dotted quad or dotted decimal notation*. Each of the four groups contains a one- to three-digit number. The number in each group is significant. IP addresses are not created at random. Starting from the left side, each group is used to narrow a computer's search for your computer on the physical network.

The three-digit number in each group is known as an *octet* and can have values between 0 and 255, allowing for 256 possibilities for each octet.

The dotted quad IP address is written as follows:

192.168.155.4

Each section of the address is converted to a binary number by the computer. For example, the decimal value 192 is written 11000000 as a binary value.

Subnet Masks

Addressing computers on a network requires not only an IP address but a special 32-bit number that looks similar to an IP address, called a *subnet mask*. This special number helps a network figure out whether a computer is connected to your home network or a remote network.

Determining the right subnet mask is a bit of an art form—understanding how subnetting works will help you. The following is an example of a common subnet mask:

255.255.255.0

Each 255 in the mask above converts to 11111111 binary. Therefore, the mask 255.255.255.0 really looks like this to the computer:

11111111.11111111.11111111.00000000

This number works in conjunction with the binary value of your IP address. The following is an example in which the top number represents the subnet mask and the bottom number represents the IP address 192.168.123.4:

11111111.11111111.11111111.00000000
11000000.10101000.01111011.00000100

The first three blocks of numbers (24 bits) of the subnet mask represent the network address and the last eight bits represent the host (your computer's) address.

Your computer uses a special type of arithmetic to analyze numbers written in binary code, called Boolean arithmetic. Rather than add these numbers together, a special AND operation is performed. Here is how an AND operation works:

0 AND 0 = 0
0 AND 1 = 0

1 AND 0 = 0

1 AND 1 = 1

The following is the result of an AND operation between the IP address and subnet mask in the previous example:

11111111.11111111.11111111.00000000

11000000.10101000.01111011.00000100

------------------------------------- AND

11000000.10101000.01111011.00000000

Only the first three blocks of numbers represent the network address. This means that this network will receive and deliver packets bound for any of the hosts (computers) identified as having IP addresses that fall between 0 and 255 in the last (fourth) block of numbers. The 255.255.255.0 subnet mask defines a Class C network. The next section explains the classes of networks. You can create smaller networks, essentially splitting up this Class C or other class of network by modifying the numbers in the subnet mask (see Table 5.1). You can change the significance of any of these blocks by changing them from 255 or 0 to some other significant number. For example:

0   = 00000000

64   = 01000000

128 = 10000000

192 = 11000000

A subnet mask of 255.255.255.192 would look like this:

1111111.11111111.1111111.11000000

Table 5.1 Subnets for a Class C Network

Number of Bits	Mask	Available Subnets	Available Addresses
2	255.255.255.192	2	62
3	255.255.255.224	6	30
4	255.255.255.240	14	14
5	255.255.255.248	30	6
6	255.255.255.252	62	2

Internet RFC 1878 describes subnet masks and subnetting for TCP/IP networks. You can view a copy of this RFC at *http://www.ietf.org/rfc/rfc1878.txt.*

Network Classes

Networks classes are based on the size of a network. The size is determined by how many computers can physically connect to it. You have seen how subnet masks can create networks of different sizes by altering the network address.

There are five classes of networks ranging from A to E. The Internet primarily makes use of Class A, B, and C networks. Classes D and E are generally not used by the public.

You can identify the class of network by analyzing the IP address's subnet mask used on the network or by looking at the first number in an IP address. Class A networks have a subnet mask of 255.0.0.0 and use from 0 to 126 as the value in the first octet in the IP address.

Class B networks have a subnet mask of 255.255.0.0. In a class B network, the first two octets are used (considered significant) to identify the network, meaning that there are more significant digits used when comparing an IP address against this subnet mask. More significant digits means that there are more possible class B networks. Looking at the first octet of the IP address, you will see a number between 128 and 191.

A Class C network uses a subnet mask (as described previously) of 255.255.255.0. The first octet of the IP address will have a number between 192 and 223 inclusive.

Network classes are also described in more detail in Chapter 7.

Default Gateways

Your home network may or may not have a need to communicate with the Internet. You can have a home network to share printers, hard drives, play network games, or any number of different reasons. Connecting to the Internet, however, is one of the most common reasons for creating a home network.

When your home network needs to communicate with other computers on the Internet, you will need to designate a default gateway. This can be a computer or a piece of equipment called a router.

The default gateway does an analysis of the IP address in the packets of all network traffic. Matching the IP address against the subnet mask allows the default gateway to determine if the packet is destined for a computer on your local network or should be sent out to the Internet.

When packets are destined for a local computer, the local Network Address Table (NAT) is consulted and the traffic is sent to the appropriate NIC. When the traffic is destined for the Internet, the router or gateway machine must direct the packets to the correct subnet on the Internet.

Your IP Address and You

There are times when you may need to know your computer's IP address. There are several ways to find a computer's IP address, but the following sections describe some of the simplest ways to access this information.

IP addresses and Windows 95, 98, and ME

If you use Windows 95, 98, or Millennium (Me) you can follow these steps to view your computer's IP address:

1. Click on the Start button.

2. Click on Run.

3. In the box marked Open, type:

   ```
   winipcfg
   ```

4. Click OK.

A new window will open, showing your current IP address, subnet mask, default gateway address, and other options. See Figure 5.1.

You can also access the winipcfg.exe utility from the C:\Windows or C:\Win directory on your computer.

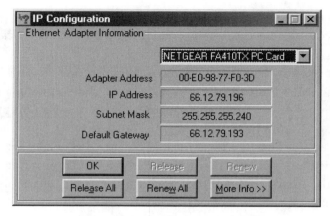

Figure 5.1 *The IP Configuration window will display your IP address.*

IP Addresses and Windows NT and 2000

If you use Windows NT or 2000, do the following to view your computer's IP address:

1. Click on the Start button.
2. Select Programs.
3. Select Command Prompt.
4. At the command prompt, type the following command and hit Enter.

   ```
   ipconfig /all
   ```

The following is an example of what the results of running **ipconfig** look like:

```
Windows 2000 IP Configuration


    Host Name . . . . . . . . . . . . : inspiron
    Primary DNS Suffix  . . . . . . . : host.tedcoombs.com
    Node Type . . . . . . . . . . . . : Hybrid

    IP Routing Enabled. . . . . . . . : No

    WINS Proxy Enabled. . . . . . . . : No
```

```
DNS Suffix Search List. . . . . . : host.tedcoombs.com
                                     tedcoombs.com


Ethernet adapter Local Area Connection:


Connection-specific DNS Suffix  . :
Description . . . . . . . . . . . : 3Com EtherLink XL
   10/100 NIC
Physical Address. . . . . . . . . : 00-10-06-CA-32-BC


DHCP Enabled. . . . . . . . . . . : No


IP Address. . . . . . . . . . . . : 192.168.127.195


Subnet Mask . . . . . . . . . . . : 255.255.255.240


Default Gateway . . . . . . . . . : 192.168.127.193


DNS Servers . . . . . . . . . . . : 209.235.107.14
```

Note: If you encounter a message that tells you that **ipconfig** could not be found, it is likely that you do not have TCP/IP networking installed on your computer. You will need to follow the instructions described later in this chapter for installing TCP/IP.

IP Addresses and Windows XP

If you use Windows XP and connect to a broadband connection such as cable or DSL, you can view your IP address by following these two steps:

1. Click Start.
2. Go to My Network Places and left-click (see Figure 5.2).
3. Once you have opened the My Network Places window, select View network connections. Figure 5.3 gives you an idea of what you should see.

Figure 5.2 *Select My Network Places from your Start menu.*

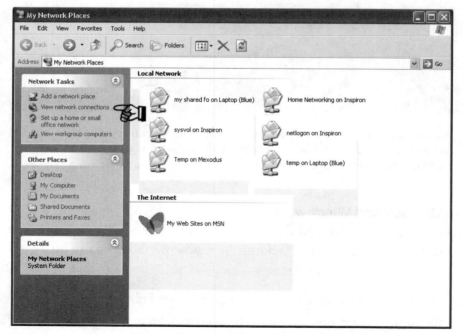

Figure 5.3 *Click on View network connections.*

Once you select View network connections, the Network Connections window will launch. To the right of the window you can view your computer's current network connections.

Left-click on the network connection in the list for which you want to view your computer's IP address. You will be able to view your IP address on the left side of the window. The Detail section on the right lists important connection information, including your computer's IP address (refer to Figure 5.4).

IP addresses and Macintosh Computers

Configuring the IP address on a Macintosh computer is slightly different than on a computer running Windows. All of the TCP/IP concepts remain the same—only the steps to view or configure the computer are different. Follow these steps:

1. From the Apple menu select Control Panels.

2. Select TCP/IP.

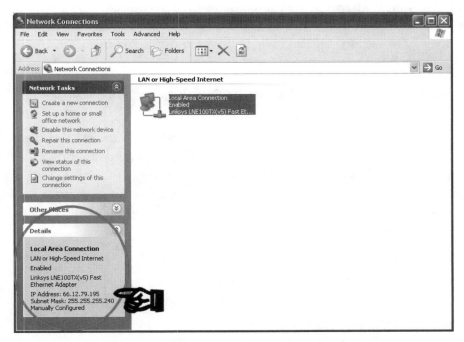

Figure 5.4 *See your IP address Details section of the Network Connections window using Windows XP.*

The TCP/IP control panel will launch and allow you to modify or view your computer's IP address.

If your computer is running the OS X operating system, the steps are slightly different. Follow these steps:

1. From the Dock or the Apple menu select System Preferences.
2. Click on Network.
3. Choose Ethernet or Modem Connection—your selection here is dependent on the connection type you are using to connect to the Internet.

The window that launches will allow you to change or view your computer's IP address.

Network Setup in Windows 95, 98, Me and 2000

Every version of Microsoft Windows has its own network setup variations. It is not guaranteed that your version of Windows will be covered in this book—you may have to refer to Windows Help for more information on modifying your network setup. You can access Help from the Start menu.

Note: You might need the Windows CD-ROM to install some of the network components.

Windows uses TCP/IP protocol to talk with other Windows-running computers on a network. You will need to install TCP/IP and configure it for your computer to communicate on the network. There are also several other optional components that, once installed, will allow your computer to share printers, files, hard drives, CD-ROMS, and more. The following are some of the various network components:

- Internet Protocol (TCP/IP)
- Client for Microsoft Networks (optional)
- File and Printer Sharing for Microsoft Windows (optional)
- NetBEUI Protocol (optional)

- AppleTalk protocol (optional for communicating with Apple machines on your network from a Windows machine)
- Microsoft DLC Protocol (optional and not recommended for home networks and not available for Windows ME)—this protocol is primarily used for communications with mainframe computers on your network

TCP/IP

TCP/IP is required for most network types. There are network types other than TCP/IP, but the chance that the home network you are installing uses a type other than TCP/IP is slim to none.

Client for Microsoft Networks

Client for Microsoft Networks is required if you want the ability to connect to other computers on your network running Windows. Connecting to these computers will allow you to share printers and files. In the case of networks with computers running server software such as Windows 2000 Server or the older Windows NT Server, you will be able to take advantage of centralized login and security as well as any other server-provided features.

File and Printer Sharing

Install the File and Printer Sharing service to either share a printer on your computer or to use a printer shared on another computer on your network. You will need to install this service to allow sharing of hard drives and files using Network Neighborhood.

NetBEUI

NetBEUI (NetBios Extended User Interface) is the network protocol used by all Windows operating systems. According to a Microsoft TechNet article, it was the earliest network protocol used to create a network of personal computers. It was designed around (and is often confused with) NetBIOS. NetBIOS is a programming interface that allows programs to extend your computer's BIOS to allow networking features.

For more information on NetBEUI, read the following Microsoft TechNet article:

http://www.microsoft.com/technet/treeview/default.asp?url=/TechNet/prodtech-nol/winntas/support/sur_nbf.asp?frame=true

---

Mini Network Components Glossary

Client software: Lets you use files and printers that are shared on the networks.

Adapter: The device in your computer that is physically connecting your computer to the network (e.g. network card).

Protocols: Language that the computer uses to communicate with other computers. Most computers use the same language or protocols to communicate correctly with each other. (e.g. Http, IC\IP, etc.)

Services: Lets you share you files and printers with other computers on the network. System backup, remote registry, and network monitor agents are types of services.

Installing Network Components

To install network components described or modify your network setup, do the following steps. If you have not already installed your NIC, you will need the correct driver software available from the NIC manufacturer. You should install your NIC before continuing with any other network setup. Note that if you use Windows 2000, you will need to take different steps (these will follow).

1. Click the Start button.
2. Select Settings.
3. Click Control Panel.
4. Double-click the Network icon.
5. In Windows 95, 98, and ME, the Network window will appear with the name of the network components installed in your computer.

To set up networking components on Windows 2000, follow these steps:

1. Follow step 1 through 3 from the previous list.
2. Click the Network and Dial-up Connection icon.
3. After the window appears, click the icon labeled Local Area Connection.
4. Click Properties and the Local Area Connection Properties window will launch.

The Local Area Connection Properties window lists the various networking components currently in use by your computer. It is possible that none will appear if you have never used your computer on a network.

Click the Install button to add a new component. This will launch the Network Component Type window. You can then choose to install a Client, Service, or Protocol by clicking the corresponding icon and then clicking the Add button.

A list of available components will appear for each specific network component type. Select the component you would like to install and click the OK button. If the component you would like to install is not included in the list and you have the software for this component on a disk, click the Have Disk button, specify the location of the software, and click OK. The components available on the disk will appear in a list. Select the component from the list and click OK. The component will then install.

Once you have installed a network component, most versions of Microsoft Windows will need to reboot before the component can be used.

Setting up a Wireless Network Card

Setting up a wireless network card requires a few more steps than setting up a wired NIC. Wireless networking requires that you configure communications between the wireless NIC and the access-point hardware.

Start the software that came with your wireless network card. While editing the configuration you should find a place to set the communications channel. It may simply be labeled Channel. This should be set to the channel your access-point hardware is configured to use.

Note: Some wireless networks automatically scan all channels until a communication channel is found, and set the channel automatically. The equipment will connect to the proper equipment by matching a special Extended Service Set Identifier (ESSID).

Your software may require that you set the ESSID to match that of the access point. The program may also have a scan feature that finds all available access points and allows you to select the access point to which you would like to connect, setting the ESSID automatically. There may also be a feature that allows your network card to connect to any ESSID. This is particularly useful if your computer is mobile and you expect it to connect to foreign (installed somewhere other than your home) networks.

If your network requires that you set the network type of mode, the setting is normally set to Infrastructure. You can also choose to have communications over your network encrypted. Remember that your wireless network communications do not necessarily end at the walls or roof. Some of your network communications may escape outside and be intercepted by anyone with the capability to do so. Encrypting network communications protects the privacy of your communications.

Domain Names

This chapter has covered a great deal of information about IP addresses. After the initial setup of your home network, you rarely have to think about your network or computer's IP address. Domain names are aliases for Internet IP addresses. Can you imagine 66.218.71.86 written on the side of a bus instead of Yahoo!? Each domain name represents an IP address to make referencing Internet sites easier for people to remember and use.

Domain names are made up of three parts; the host, the domain, and the top-level domain. The following is the analysis of the domain name *www.digitalmarketplace.com*:

In this example, **www** is the host name, **digitalmarketplace** is the domain, and **com** is the top-level domain. Note that **www** is only one possible host name—you can call your computer anything you wish.

These three parts of a domain name are known collectively as a *Fully Qualified Domain Name* (FQDN). The host name represents the name of the computer, or one of its aliases, hosting the server software providing the resource you are referencing. The domain is the name of the network on which the resource resides and the top-level domain identifies the type of resource. There are many top-level domains and new ones are created every day. The following are some of the top-level domains available presently:

- Com   Commercial
- Edu   Educational
- Gov   Governmental
- Org   Non-profit organization
- Biz   Business
- Info   Informational

DNS works in a tree-shaped hierarchy, with each level of the tree providing a different level of authoritative responsibility for knowing the IP address corresponding to a domain name. The top of the tree is the domain name registrar. This is the organization or company you use to register your domain name. The following explains how DNS works in a little more detail.

Your ISP runs a name server (DNS server) that matches your FQDN with a particular IP address. If you obtain your IP address using DHCP, the DHCP server can contact the DNS server program and update your FQDN with the IP address you have most recently been issued. But, this is not enough to know how to locate your computer using a domain name. When someone wants to contact your computer using a domain name, they must first know how to find the name server that knows your IP address. When you register your domain name you include the network address of the DNS servers that are responsible for knowing your IP address. So, the lookup sequence goes like this. A computer wants to contact your computer by FQDN. This computer contacts the domain name registrar and asks it what name servers are responsible for knowing your computer's IP address. The registrar gives the IP address of the name server. The computer then contacts the name server and asks for your computer's IP address. The name server sends your IP address to the computer trying to contact your computer. Once that computer has your IP address it can communicate directly with your computer. So, the chain (or hierarchy) of information is important to the operation of the domain name system.

Domain Name Registrars

Domain name registrars allow you to register a domain name. When you register a domain name, you register the domain and top-level domain parts of a domain name, but not the host name. You also register the names of the computers that will provide you with actual DNS service. This will be discussed in greater detail in the next section.

 Note: Your DNS provider, not the domain name registrar, is responsible for mapping host names such as www to IP addresses.

Domain name registrars vary based on cost and quality of service. GoDaddy.com is an example of a good registrar. It provides excellent service and one of the lowest registration fees. Visit *http://www.godaddy.com* for more information.

DNS Servers

Domain names are managed by DNSs. Each DNS is responsible for managing domain names and the IP addresses associated with the domain name and hosts in the domain. Once the information is entered by the administrator of a DNS server, it is available to be queried. The following is a typical example.

I enter *www.digitalmarketplace.com* into my Web browser. My computer needs to know the IP address of the Web server at *www.digitalmarketplace.com*. My computer contacts the DNS server I have entered into my network information, or by default the DNS server of my ISP.

If *www.digitalmarketplace.com* happens to be managed by the same DNS server your computer uses to look up domain names, your computer will be sent the correct IP address immediately. If your DNS server has recently looked up *www.digitalmarketplace.com* and has the IP address in its cache, the IP address will also be returned immediatly to your Web browser. This is because the DNS server you use to lookup the domain name also happens to be the authoritative name server for *digitalmarketplace.com*.

Chances are high that *www.digitalmarketplace.com* will not be managed by your ISP's name server. Therefore the DNS server run by your ISP will contact a central domain name registry to find out who the authoritative name server is for *www.digitalmarketplace.com*. The DNS server then contacts the authoritative name server, retrieves the IP address, places it in the cache and sends it to my Web browser. In the event the primary authoritative name server is not operating, the backup authoritative name server is queried. This all happens within seconds.

Name server cache can be a bit of a problem. If you ever change your name server or domain name information it may take two days to a week until most of the name servers have flushed their cache and have the most current information. Until then, people trying to contact you by IP address may not reach you.

Your ISP may provide you with free DNS hosting or may choose to charge you a one-time or annual fee for domain hosting. It is not necessary to use the DNS server belonging to your ISP. Any name server anywhere in the world can provide you with name service. A good commercial name service is provided by Digital Marketplace, Inc. Visit *www.digitalmarketplace.com* to receive free or commercial DNS service for your domain name.

Summary

Setting up your network software can be the most challenging part of your network installation. There are many options: internal vs. Internet IP addresses; DHCP-distributed, dynamic IP addresses vs. static IP addresses; and a number of security, routing, and domain name options. This chapter described each of these possible selections. Of course, the manual that comes with your network should also help you configure this network information.

Network Sharing

6

The first use of computer networks was to share printers between mainframe computers. Companies installed networks when they had several mainframe computers and wanted them all to print to a single high-speed printer. Your home network has this same ability to share printers and much more. This chapter will act as a guide for configuring the computers on your network to share files, hard drives, and peripherals such as printers.

Some useful hints are given about sharing the printer so that MS-DOS applications as well as Windows programs can make use of it. We also explain how the Microsoft Network Neighborhood allows files and applications to be shared over the Internet. Also introduced in this chapter are Web folders for sharing files across the Internet.

Getting Started

Networks have resources. These resources are considered anything shared by a computer attached to the network. These resources can be printers, hard drives, files, and modems.

To enable network sharing of resources between computers on your network, you must first make certain that all the right software has been installed on each computer. Chapter 5 discusses software installation in detail.

Make certain you have installed the Client for Microsoft Windows and File and Printer Sharing for Microsoft Networks components as part of your network configuration. To check this, launch your network configuration as described in Chapter 5 and look for these two components. If they are not installed, follow the instructions in Chapter 5 for installing these components.

Sharing Printers

All computers on your network have the ability to share their printers. Many homes purchase a single printer and share it among all of the computers in the house. But this does not have to be the case. You may have a black and white laser printer attached to one computer and a color ink jet printer attached to another. Both computers can share their printers so that other network users can choose to which printer to send their printing output. It is also possible for a single computer to have more than one printer attached to it. You may share as many printers on your network as you can attach to your computers.

Attaching the Printer to the Computer

Connect your printer to the appropriate printer port. Printers normally attach in the following ways:

- Parallel (LPT – Line Print Terminal) port
- Serial port
- USB port
- Wireless Infrared port

Installing a printer normally involves installation of printer software commonly known as *printer drivers*. Follow the manufacturer's instructions for installing the drivers and test the printer. Once you are certain that the printer is functioning correctly with the computer to which it is attached, you can move to the next step—sharing the computer with others over the network.

Configuring Printer Sharing

There are two things that you must do to share your printer. First, configure sharing on the computer to which the printer is attached. Second, configure other computers on the network to use this shared printer. The shared printer or printers are commonly known as *network printers*.

Note: Some printers require that you install the same driver software on both the computer to which the printer is attached and the other computer using the shared printer.

Configuring the Print Server

The computer to which the printer is attached is known in the world of networks as the *print server*. The print server has two functions. It physically provides the printer over the network and also allows data destined for the printer to spool into a print queue. The print queue keeps track of all documents bound for the shared printer.

Once you have shared a printer, you will be able to make use of this printer from other computers. You will first have to configure the computer to use the shared printer.

Windows 95, 98, and Me Print Servers

If your computer is running Windows 95, 98, or Me, the printer should be installed on the print server as follows:

1. Click the Start button.

2. Select Settings.

3. Click on Printers and a new window will open displaying the installed printers.

4. Right–click on the printer you wish to share.

5. From the popup menu select Sharing… The printer's Properties window will launch.

6. In the Printer Properties window, make certain the Sharing tab has been selected. Click the Shared As option.

7. Once you have selected the Shared As option, a default name for your printer will appear in the textbox next to this option. You may choose to keep this name or enter a new name for your printer by overwriting the default name.

8. Clicking the General tab in the Printer Properties window will allow you to enter a location and comment that describes the printer you are sharing. This is useful when many printers are shared. For example, the location could be Mom's Room, or Den. The comment could describe the printer in more detail such as, photo-quality color-ink jet.

9. Click the OK button when you have finished configuring the printer for sharing. The icon that represents your printer will change to show a hand with the printer letting you know that you are sharing this printer. The hand is a common symbol for sharing in Microsoft network software.

Windows 2000 and Windows XP Print Servers

The steps for sharing printers on a computer running Windows 2000 or Windows XP are similar to those described for Windows 95, 98, and Me. Figure 6.1 and Figure 6.2 demonstrate the steps for sharing printers and using network printers in a Windows XP environment.

Configure your computer to be a print server by following these steps:

1. Click Start and select Printers and Faxes.

2. Right-click on the printer you want to share. Then click Sharing... This will launch the Printer Properties window.

3. In the Printer Properties window you should be in the Sharing tab. Select Share this printer..., as shown in Figure 6.2.

4. Type a share name for your printer and click the OK button.

The printer is now shared and available over the network.

Figure 6.1 *Select Sharing ... from the menu.*

Figure 6.2 *Configure sharing in the Printer Properties window.*

Configuring your Computer to Use a Shared Printer

When you use a printer that has been shared over the network, it will appear as though you have a printer directly attached to your computer. Software that allows you to print will list shared printers in the same way it will list printers attached to your computer. The following sections describe how to share a printer, depending on which Windows version you use.

Windows 95, 98, and Me Network Printing

If you use Windows 95, 98, or Me computers and would like to share a printer, follow these steps:

1. Double click the Network Neighborhood icon on your computer desktop or open Windows Explorer.

2. Browse the Network Neighborhood to find the computer that is sharing the printer.

3. Once you have found the computer, click on it to access the resources that are shared by that computer.

4. You should be able to see the shared printer—right-click on it.

5. From the popup menu select Install.

6. The Add Printer Wizard will launch.

7. The first page of the wizard will ask you if you print from MS-DOS programs. (Most users only print from Windows.) A safe choice is No. Click Next.

8. The Add Printer Wizard will ask, How is this printer attached to your computer? Select Network Printer and click Next.

9. The next page of the wizard asks for the printer make and model. Select your printer make and model from the list. If your printer is not in the list or if you have the drivers on a disk, click the Have a Disk button. Browse to where the drivers are located on your hard drive, CD, or diskette.

10. Once you have selected the correct make and model of your printer, click Next.

11. If a driver was already installed for the printer, the wizard will ask you if you want to keep the existing driver or replace it. If you are certain this is the correct driver, select Keep existing driver. If you have a newer version of the printer driver you should select Replace existing driver. Click Next to continue.

12. Type a name for the network printer. For example, you can type Deskjet932 or any other name that would best describe that particular printer. Click Next.

You should be able to use the printer now.

Windows 2000 or Windows XP Network Printing

Follow these steps to begin using a network printer on a computer running either Windows 2000 or Windows XP:

1. For Windows XP click Start and then click Printers and Faxes. For Windows 2000 click Start, Settings, and then Printers.

2. Select Add a Printer.

3. When the Add a Printer Wizard launches, click Next to start the Wizard (Figure 6.3).

4. Select either Local printer attached to this computer or A network printer (a printer attached to another computer). Click Next to continue.

5. Specify a Printer (Figure 6.4) If you know how to write out the full name of the print server and printer you can enter it in the Name field. You can also enter the printer as a URL. If these methods are foreign to you, it is easiest to select Browse for a Printer. The Name field will then be automatically filled in correctly when you select a printer. When you have finished selecting a printer, click Next.

6. If you have chosen to browse for a printer, you can locate the printer you would like to use through Network Neighborhood. (Figure 6.5) Once you find it, click on it and then click Next.

7. The last question the wizard asks you is whether you want this printer to be the default printer. Selecting this printer to be the default printer means that this printer will be selected by default when you choose to print. You can always override the default and select another printer (Figure 6.6). Select a choice and then click Next.

8. If your selection was successful, the wizard will display information about the selected printer. (Figure 6.7) Click the Finish button to complete the wizard.

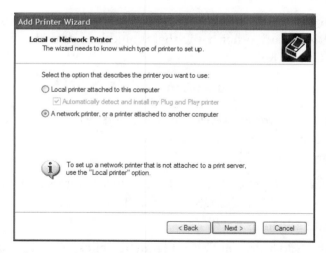

Figure 6.3 *Select the type of printer in the Printer Wizard window.*

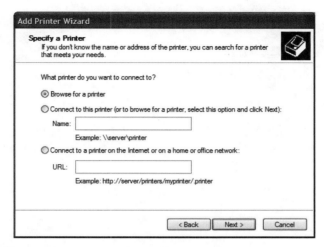

Figure 6.4 *Browse for the printer or type the name or URL.*

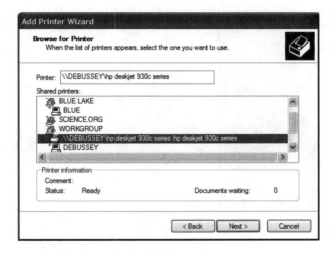

Figure 6.5 *Locate the printer and then click Next.*

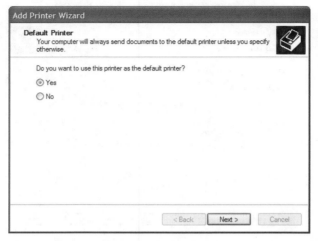

Figure 6.6 *Specify if you want this printer to be the default printer.*

Figure 6.7 *The wizard displays information about the selected printer.*

Naming Your Printer

It is important to give your printer a meaningful name. If you have more than one printer on the network, then how you name each one becomes even more important. A good name will clearly identify a printer.

Some operating systems allow longer names for your printer than others. You must be careful that the name you specify on your computer will also be acceptable on other computers on your network. For example, Windows 2000 and higher accept names longer than 32 characters but other Windows operating systems accept fewer than 32 characters. Keep in mind that older MS-DOS programs will identify printers with 8 or fewer characters in the printer name. The restriction on the length of the printer name is not always a factor of the operating system; some older programs have length restrictions on printer names as well.

A good way to name your printer would be to identify the make and model; for example, if you have a Hewlett Packard LaserJet 4550 Color laser printer, you can call it HPLaserJet. If you have two printers that are the same brand/model and located in the same room, just add a number after the name like, HpLaserJet01 and HPLaserJet02.

You might also consider adding a comment to your printer definition. This will make identifying your printer simpler. You can add a comment by going to the printer properties and following these steps:

1. Click Start.
2. Select Control Panel.
3. Select Printers and Faxes.
4. Right-click on the printer to which you would like to add a comment. You will find the comment in the General tab.

In some operating systems you can also specify a location for your printer. This may help further identify your printer (Figure 6.8).

Printer Drivers

The printer's drivers are the software that allow your computer and printer to communicate. When you buy a printer, most of the drivers will be included on a diskette or CD-ROM.

Some printers require that you install the drivers while installing the printer support software. This often allows advanced configuration features to become available.

Figure 6.8 *Type the location and a comment to make it easier to identify your printer on the network.*

If you lose the driver software for your printer, contact the manufacturer. Most companies make the software available for download from their Web site—you can be certain that the most recent drivers will be available.

Sharing Folders and Files

Folders are the mechanisms for organizing files on a storage disk such as a hard drive, CD-ROM, DVD-ROM, diskette, or other disk-based storage medium. Almost all computer programs and data is stored in files and files are stored in folders. You may see folders also referred to by older terminology, such as *directories*.

When you share folders on the network, you allow others to have access to the files stored in the folders. Sharing a folder normally shares any subfolders. A subfolder is a folder created within another folder to further organize files. The entire folder mechanism is structured in a tree shape. The root of the tree is the root folder. When you share the root folder, you share the entire disk.

For security reasons, sharing an entire hard drive is not recommended. This is particularly true if you are allowing full control of all the files on the hard drive. Some folders should not be shared, such as the Windows folders that contain your computer's system files and information that allows your computer to function correctly. Sharing system folders opens your computer to accidental or malicious damage to files important to your operating system.

Be particular about the folders you share. We recommend that you create a folder particularly designed for sharing files. In this manner, you can control which files are placed in this folder and not open up more of your computer's hard drive than is necessary. You can then choose to allow several levels of access to the folder. You can choose to allow others to read files only, write files only, or both read and write files. Additional levels of security will also allow others to delete files from this directory.

Sharing Folders on Windows 95, 98, and Me

The procedure to share a folder is very similar across all versions of Windows. The following steps will allow you to share a folder on Windows 95, 98, and Me.

1. Find the My Computer icon on the desktop and double-click on it or open Windows Explorer.

2. Browse for the drive or folder you want to share.

3. Right-click the item to be shared and select Sharing from the popup menu (see Figure 6.9).

4. Once the folder's Properties windows opens, select the Sharing tab.

5. Select Share As by clicking the corresponding radio button (see Figure 6.10).

6. Type a name for the shared folder and add an optional comment. You can choose to use the default name of the folder or share the folder under a different name. For example, the folder might be named My Documents. Renaming it to Mary's Documents will make the contents more obvious on the network. Sharing a folder under a different name will not change how that folder appears on the local hard drive.

7. If the Shared-level Access Control is activated, select an Access Type. With Read-Only, the users will be able access files and open them but would not be able to save changes. With Full, users have complete control of the folder—they can add files or folders, make changes to the files in the folder, and even erase existing files or folders. The last option requires that the user enter a password. You will need to enter the users who have full access or assign a password for full control.

8. If you want to password-protect the folders, type a password in the Passwords section of the folder's Properties window textbox. You can specify a different password for each of the Access Types you have allowed for this folder. Not specifying a password allows free access to these folders.

Saving the folder properties will immediately share your folder. The folder should appear in the Windows Explorer with a hand beneath it, designating that it is shared.

There are different types of sharing depending on the Windows version you are using. Windows 2000, for instance, has Classic File Sharing while Windows XP Professional has both Simple File Sharing and Classic File Sharing.

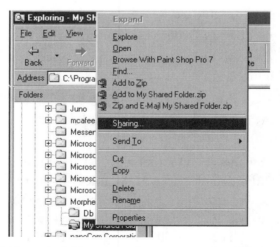

Figure 6.9 *Right-clicking on a folder name allows you to select Sharing.*

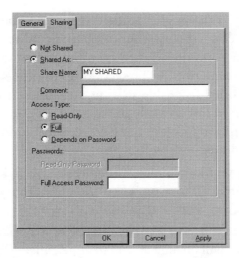

Figure 6.10 *You can change the name or leave the current name of the shared folder.*

Simple File Sharing on Windows XP

Simple file sharing is very similar to the type of sharing that is a part of Windows 95, 98, and Me. The difference is that when you enable File Sharing on Windows XP, you also enable the Guest account. This means that the person that accesses your folder from your network will have the same privileges as the Guest account user when accessing your computer. The Guest account is used by people that do not have an individual account on the computer. The Guest account can only perform limited jobs such as playing games, browsing the Internet, and word processing. This account has limited access to folders and files and in most cases access is read-only. Simple file sharing is based only on passwords that grant or restrict access (Read-only or Full access).

Follow the next steps to share files and drives on Windows XP for the first time:

1. Click on the My Computer icon on the desktop or open Windows Explorer.

2. Browse for the drive or folder you want to share. Highlight the item to be shared and right-click, launching the popup menu. Select Sharing and Security... (see Figure 6.11).

3. Figure 6.12 shows the properties for the folder to be shared. The first set of properties is concerned with local sharing and security. Local sharing is used when your computer is used by more than one person, each with their own login and profile. The second set of properties is for network sharing and security. To enable sharing, you must choose one of the two links that appear in this area. If you have not yet configured your network, click the first link to do so. If you have already configured the network, click the second link. This will bypass the Network Setup Wizard.

4. When the new window launches (Figure 6.13), click the second radio button, Just enable file sharing. Then click OK. You will not want to run the Network Setup Wizard at this time.

5. The Network sharing and security section of the Sharing tab on the folder Properties dialog will change a little in appearance (Figure 6.14). To share the folder, simply check the box labeled Share this folder on the Network.

6. Once you check the box in Step 5, the box beneath it, Allow network users to change my files, will appear checked. This means that you are giving full control of the folder or drive to other users on the network. To make the folder read-only, uncheck that box.

By following these steps, you enable the Guest account and remove it from the list of accounts that are denied access to this computer from the network. You can change the Guest account permissions to limit or increase the level of accessibility to files.

The Create Shared Folder Wizard

For Windows 2000 and Windows XP users, there is another way to create shared folders. You can use the Create Shared Folder Wizard. It is fast and easy to use. From the Start menu, select Run or open the Command Prompt.

Type shrpubw and hit Enter to start the wizard. Browse your computer for the folder you want to share. Type a name and description of the folder, then click Next.

The wizard will then prompt you to set the permissions for file access by network users. Click Finish to complete your sharing setup. The wizard will ask you if you want to share another folder. You can continue sharing folders until you have finished, then simply respond No and the wizard will complete.

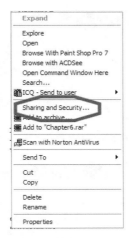

Figure 6.11 *Select Sharing and Security... located in the middle of the menu.*

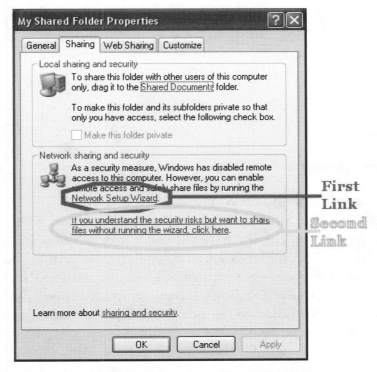

Figure 6.12 *Select the Sharing tab on the folder's Properties window to share a folder. Select Sharing and Security... located in the middle of the menu.*

Figure 6.13 *Simply enable the File Sharing window or use a Wizard to configure file sharing.*

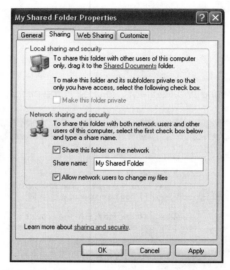

Figure 6.14 *The folder's Properties window changes after the file sharing is enabled.*

Classic File Sharing on Windows 2000 and XP

With Classic File Sharing (Windows 2000 and Windows XP), you have greater control over who can make use of which folder or files. Classic File Sharing security is based on permissions. The properties of each file contain information about the permissions granted based on users and groups.

To activate Classic File Sharing on a computer running Windows XP, start the Control Panel and double-click Folder Options. In the Folder Options dialog, click the View tab. Scroll through the Advance Settings and uncheck the last box—Use Simple File Sharing (Recommended). Figure 6.15 shows the box you have to uncheck. To finish this process, click the OK button.

Once Classic File Sharing has been activated, whenever you select the Sharing and Security tab of the folder you want to share, you will see that it looks different than it does with Simple File Sharing (see Figure 6.16). You can give the folder a different share name and add a comment. You can also specify the number of users that can connect to that folder simultaneously.

By employing Classic File Sharing you will grant access only to persons that have an account on that computer or who are allowed to log into the computer using the Guest account. When you log into Windows XP or Windows 2000, you must specify a user name and password. This user name is used to identify you on the network. For example, you may be logged into your office computer and want to connect to a computer in your child's room. You must have an account on your child's computer in order to gain access. The name of the account on your child's computer must match the user name you used when logging into your own office computer. You will be granted permission to files on both computers based on the permissions given to your user name.

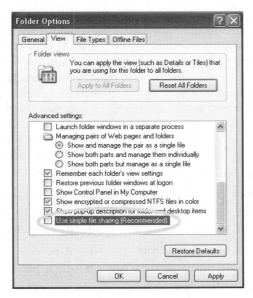

Figure 6.15 *Uncheck the last box of the Folder Options window.*

Figure 6.16 *The Sharing tab on the folder's Properties window.*

Note: It is recommended that you add all users of the home network with which you expect to share peripherals, files, and folders to your machine, even if they never physically use your computer. Adding their user accounts will allow you to control their access to resources by setting the permissions for this account. The simplest way to add users is by typing "control userpasswords2" in the Run Command. Remember to also specify passwords for your new users.

If you simply share the folder without specifying permissions, everyone on the network will have full control by default. By explicitly setting permissions, you can specify who has full control or read-only access. You can also limit file access to a single person on the network. Click on the Permissions button to control the folder's permissions.

The Caching button allows you to specify how the file will be managed while other members of the network are accessing them. You will notice that after you click the Apply button a new button will appear beneath the Caching button. The function of the New Share button is to create another share of the same folder.

Accessing Shared Folders

So far in this chapter, you have seen how it is possible to share folders on your computer with others. You may also want to use files shared on someone else's computer.

To access shared folders on another computer, first open Windows Explorer. Select Network Neighborhood or Network Places (depending on your Windows version). Within either Network Neighborhood or Network Places you will see a list of all computers on your network within the same workgroup. Workgroups are groups of computers that you are most likely to communicate with on your network. Home networks generally have a single workgroup, but if you have created more than one workgroup click on Entire Network and you will see the names of all workgroups.

Note: More advanced network settings allow you to have more than one domain on your network. Each domain will show up as a workgroup in your Network Neighborhood.

Double-clicking on the computer that contains the files you wish to share will display a list of folders currently shared by that computer. You may access these folders as you would any folder on your local computer. Depending on the type of security and permissions set for the folder, you may be asked to enter a user name and password when selecting a folder.

Depending on your permission limits, you will be able to treat this folder as you would a local folder—accessing , creating, copying, pasting, and deleting files.

File Sharing on the Macintosh

There are two file-sharing protocols for Apple Macintosh computers.

- AppleTalk (AT) – This is the classic method for sharing files, and it has been available since the early days of the Macintosh.

- Apple Filing Protocol – This protocol was introduced in the Mac OS 9 operating system. Unlike AT, this protocol will let you share files over the Internet.

To share your files, you must first configure your Macintosh computer for file sharing.

Configuring a Macintosh for File Sharing

It is not difficult to configure a Macintosh for file sharing. Follow these steps:

1. From the Apple menu, select Control Panels and click the Sharing Setup icon.

2. Enter your user name.

3. Enter your password. This will allow you to log into your computer from other Macintosh computers on your network.

4. Name your computer. This will be the name others on your network see. Just like Windows computers have workgroups, Macintosh computers have AppleTalk zones. Users in the same zone will be able to see each other's computers.

5. In the section labeled File Sharing, click Start.

File sharing will now be activated on your Macintosh computer. Before anyone can have access to files on your computer they must be configured as a registered user.

Creating a Registered User

Only registered users can access shared files. You must first create a new registered user and then grant them access to your files. Follow these steps to create a registered user:

1. From the Apple menu, select Choose Control Panels and open the Users and Groups icon.

2. When you choose New User from the File menu, a New User icon will appear selected and ready for editing.

3. Enter the name of a person you want to register.

Setting the Password of a Registered User

For security reasons it is very important to set passwords for each of your registered users. Follow these steps:

1. Locate the icon of the user for which you would like to add a password, and double-click on it.
2. Enter a password in the User Password box. A password may be up to eight characters in length. Note that passwords are case sensitive.
3. Close the window and click Save in the dialog box.

Sharing a Folder or Disk

Once you have added registered users and turned on sharing, you are ready to begin sharing folders and disks. Follow these steps:

1. On your desktop, select your hard drive icon (usually designated MacHD) by clicking once on it.
2. Select Sharing from the File menu.
3. Click the box labeled Share this item and its contents.
4. Select a user from the User/Group popup menu.
5. To share the item with everyone on the network, select the Everyone box in the third row of boxes. To share with just a selected user(s), do not click any of the Everyone boxes.
6. Close the dialog and click Save.

Network Neighborhood

Microsoft Windows has a feature known as Network Neighborhood or My Network Places in newer versions. You can access the Network Neighborhood as a feature of the Windows Explorer or from the Network Neighborhood icon on your Windows desktop. The Network Neighborhood allows you to access shared resources, share them, view them, and map them. You can navigate among all of the computers on your network.

Right-clicking the desktop icon for Network Neighborhood will present you with a context menu. From this menu, you can choose to Search for Computers, Map Network Drive, and Disconnect Network Drive.

Selecting Properties from the context menu will launch the Network and Dialup Connections configuration window. In this window, you can choose to view your computer's network identification or add additional network components. These components consist of Management and Monitoring Tools, Network Services, and other Network File and Print Services.

Mapping a Network Drive

The Windows operating system allows you to use shared folders and configure them so that they appear as a separate drive within applications or in Windows Explorer. When you configure a shared folder in this manner it is known as creating a *virtual drive*. A virtual drive appears like a local hard drive, but actually accesses information out on the network.

You can configure a shared folder to appear as a virtual drive on your computer by mapping the folder to a drive letter. For example, if the host has shared the C:\My Documents folder, you can map that folder so that it appears with a drive letter on your computer. This simplifies file access and enables you to treat the host's folder as if it were a drive on your computer. For example, you can specify that the C:\My Documents folder on the host be the F drive on your computer, as follows:

1. Start Windows Explorer and choose Network Neighborhood or select Network Neighborhood from your desktop. Find the shared folder as described in the instructions for using shared folders. Highlight the shared folder you want to map by clicking once on it. Do not open that shared folder.

2. Right-click on the folder name to launch the context menu.

3. Select Map Network Drive... from the popup context menu.

4. In the Map Network Drive dialog, select the desired drive letter. All available drive letters are accessible from the drop down list. You should reserve A and B for floppy disks.

5. The folder list allows you to select or type in a path to a shared folder. If you have highlighted the folder you intend to map, this field cannot be edited.

6. The last checkbox labeled Reconnect at logon, when checked, tells Windows to attempt mapping of this folder to the selected drive letter each time you logon to your computer.

You can also map drives such as CD-ROM, DVD-ROM, or CD-R and CD-RW drives. Some software will allow you to play movies and music from mapped CD-ROMs and DVD-ROMs.

Computer Sharing

Each computer connected to your network might allow more than one user. Users on the same computer might want different folders and/or files or even different desktop themes than the other users who use the computer. Windows solves this challenge by letting you add users to the computer. Each user can have individualized folders and programs. The following is a list of features allowable by having different users:

- Protect and personalize your settings such as desktop themes.

- Each user has a personalized list of Web favorites and recently visited sites.

- Every user has a My Documents folder and can use passwords to keep it safe.

- Each program runs according to the settings in the user's preferences. For example, each user can have their own Internet Explorer start page.

- Windows XP users do not have to close programs to change users.

- Allowing multiple users enables you to determine the ownership of files and folders. For example, if user John writes a document using Microsoft Word, the document's properties will identify John as the author.

The Quick Switch

Windows XP has the ability for quick switching between users. Instead of going to the Start menu, logging off, and then switching users, you can do this by pressing the Windows logo key + L. This key combination will take you directly to the Welcome Screen where you choose the user to log in.

User profiles contain all of the information described in the bullet list above for each user. Each version of the Windows operating system manages profiles in unique ways but the end result is the same.

To add, delete, or change settings for Windows 98 and Me users, follow these steps:

1. Open the Control Panel.
2. Double click User. The User Settings window (Figure 6.17) will launch and you will be able to see a list of users that are set up for that computer.

In this User Setting window you can manage the user's password and settings. Adding a new user is very simple, just click on the New User button, and enter a user name (up to 128 characters long) and an optional password. If you leave the password space blank, anyone who uses that computer will be able to login with the user name you just created. The last step is to complete the Personalized Items Settings. Here you choose to customize the way the computer acts towards this user.

On Windows 2000, the process is a little more complex:

1. Click the Start button.
2. Select Programs.
3. Select Administrative Tools.
4. Click on Computer Management.
5. The Computer Management window will launch. Under System Tools, you should see a subcategory called Local Users and Groups.

6. Under Local Users and Groups there are two folders, one for Users and the other for Groups.

7. Begin by right-clicking on the Users folder.

8. Select New User... from the menu.

As in Windows 98, you will have to type a user name and an optional (but recommended) password. You can also enter a description about the user.

Windows XP users have the ability to use any or both of the methods described above for managing user profiles. Figure 6.18 shows the Windows XP Computer Management Window. In the Windows XP Control Panel, you will choose the User Accounts applet rather than the Windows 2000 Users applet.

As you can see from the illustration, Windows 2000 and XP have a feature known as Groups. Each user is part of one or more groups. Security and permissions for each user are set based on the groups to which the user belongs. In Table 6.1, you see the default groups created when XP Professional edition is installed and the description that Microsoft gives to each group.

Figure 6.17 *The User Settings window includes a list of the registered users.*

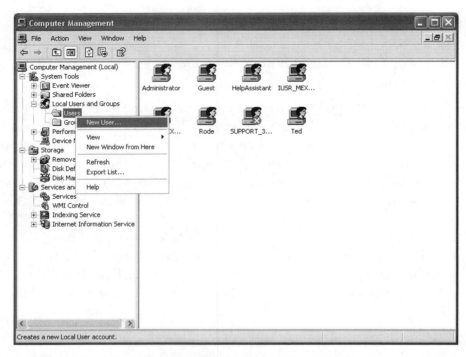

Figure 6.18 *Right click on Users and then select New User to create a new user from the Computer Management window.*

Table 6.1 Groups in Windows 2000 and XP

Group Name	Description
Administrator	Administrators have complete and unrestricted access to the computer/domain.
Backup Operators	Backup operators can override security restrictions for the sole purpose of backing up or restoring files.
Guest	Guests have the same access as members of the Users group by default, except for the Guest account which is further restricted.
Network Configuration Operators	Members in this group can have some administrative privileges to manage configuration of networking features.
Power Users	Power users possess most administrative powers with some restrictions. Power users can run legacy applications in addition to certified applications.

Table 6.1 Groups in Windows 2000 and XP *(continued)*

Group Name	Description
Remote Desktop Users	Members in this group are granted the right to log on remotely.
Replicator	The Replicator supports file replication in a domain.
Users	Users are prevented from making accidental or intentional system-wide changes. Users can run certified applications but not most legacy applications
Debugger Users	Debugger users can debug processes on this machine, both locally and remotely
HelpServicesGroup	This group is for the Help and Support Center.

By default, Windows XP allows you to designate a user as either an Administrator or Guest. You can also create new groups with custom security levels. You may then add a user to as many groups as you need. Remember that the security is additive such that if one group grants write access to a resource and another group grants read access, the user belonging to both groups will have both read and write access.

Note about Active Directory For Windows 2000 and XP: Active Directory is an advanced topic and is rarely used on home networks—but if your computer is configured as a domain controller, you are required to use Active Directory to manage your users. Refer to your operating system instructions for managing Active Directory.

Remote Desktop Connection

Today, most people have computers at home as well as at the office. Many times we take the office work home to finish it. Sometimes, we realize that we forgot a file or that we do not have all of the software we need in our computer at home to do the work we need. Windows XP has a new feature that solves this problem. With a feature called *Remote Desktop Connection* you can connect to any computer that is also running Windows XP, at least the ones you have permission to access. Remote Desktop Connect requires that you have a user name and password to connect.

Once you are connected, you can control the remote computer as though you were sitting in front of it. A window on your local desktop allows you to view the remote desktop, giving you access to all of the programs and files.

To configure the computer running Windows XP Professional to accept a Remote Connection, do the following:

1. Click the Start button.
2. Select Control Panel.
3. Start the System applet by double-clicking the System icon.
4. On the System Properties window click the Remote tab (Figure 6.19).
5. Check the box labeled Allow users to connect remotely to this computer.
6. Click Apply.

You can specify which user you want to be able to connect to this computer by clicking on Select Remote users… This allows you to add users to the Remote Desktop Users group.

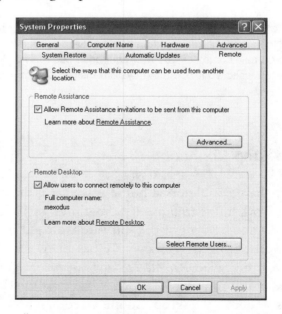

Figure 6.19 *You can allow remote users to connect to a computer from the Remote tab on the System Properties window.*

To set up a Remote Desktop Connection on a computer that is not running Windows XP Professional, you will need to install the Remote Desktop Connection software. You can download it from the Microsoft Windows XP Web site (*http://www.microsoft.com/windowsxp/default.asp*) or you can install it from the Windows XP CD-ROM.

To begin using the Remote Desktop Connection to control another computer, follow these steps:

1. Click the Start button.
2. Select Programs > Accessories > Communications.
3. Select Remote Desktop Connection.

The Remote Desktop Connection will open as shown in Figure 6.20.

If your computer is connected to the same network as the computer to which you would like to connect, simply type the name of the computer in the textbox found in the Remote Desktop Connection dialog. Other ways to connect to a remote computer are by specifying the IP address of the remote computer or by using the Remote Desktop Web Connection.

To use the Remote Desktop Web Connection, the remote computer must have the Internet Information Services (IIS) and the Remote Desktop Web Connection software installed. You can install them from the Windows XP Professional CD-ROM.

 Note: When the remote computer is behind a firewall, you will need to configure the firewall software to open port 3389 to allow access to that computer. Remote Desktop Connection uses port 3389 to make connections with other computers.

By clicking on the Options button, the Remote Desktop Connection windows will expand, allowing you to configure your connection (see Figure 6.21).

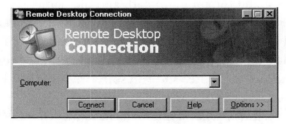

Figure 6.20 *Type the computer name or IP address to connect remotely to another computer.*

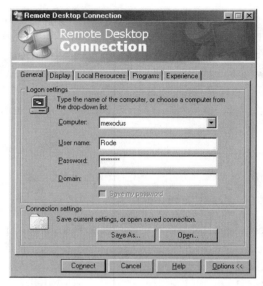

Figure 6.21 *If you are going to connect to a remote computer, add your user name and password and save your preferences.*

In the configuration's General tab, you can add your name and password. This allows you to save your settings so that the next time you want to connect, your settings will already be configured.

In the Display tab, you choose how the remote desktop is displayed, from the desktop size to the colors.

The Local Resources tab lets you configure sounds, keyboard (Windows key combinations), and local devices. You have the choice of having sounds from the remote computer played locally on your computer, remotely, or choose to have no sound at all.

If you want to start a specific program once you connect to the remote computer, you must add the program path and file name. This option will only work if you have first configured your computer as a *terminal server*. Terminal services is an advanced feature of operating systems such as Windows 2000 Server, which allow computers that are running various operating systems to connect to a Windows computer and run software programs remotely. To learn more about Terminal Services visit:

http://www.microsoft.com/windows2000/technologies/terminal/default.asp

The Experience tab has configuration options to improve performance during the connection. Depending on the speed of your network connection, different options will be checked.

Imagine that you are connecting from a home computer to an office computer. Some of the downsides may include

- You may experience slow response time—meaning it might take a little bit of time for your home computer screen to refresh or reflect your actions on your computer at work.

- Only one user can log in at the same time—meaning if you are working from home and your secretary wants to log into your computer at the same time, you will have to disconnect and reconnect at a later time.

Remote Assistant

Remote Assistant is a feature of Windows XP that allows you to provide or receive support. It uses or allows others to use your computer in a manner similar to Remote Desktop Assistant.

Just like Remote Desktop Assistant, using Remote Assistant allows you to connect to a remote computer and use it as if you were sitting in front of it. There are four main differences between Remote Assistant and Remote Desktop Connection. Some of the important differences include the following:

1. You cannot initiate a remote connection with Remote Assistant. A person using the computer you are trying to access has to invite you or ask you to use Remote Assistant. With Remote Desktop, you can connect any time, provided you have a user name and password.

2. With Remote Assistant, you do not have full control of the computer by default. You must be granted full control by the person that has asked you for assistance. You can never gain more control of a computer than what is given to the person who has invited you to provide assistance. For instance, if the person who invites you to provide assistance has guest account privileges, you will be limited to the same guest privileges.

3. With Remote Assistant, both users can view the activity on the desktop simultaneously. Remote Desktop only allows one user to see the desktop.

4. Only users with Windows XP can use Remote Assistant while Remote Desktop is available to other versions of Windows, provided you first install the appropriate software.

Requesting Remote Assistance

The easiest way to ask for help using the Remote Assistant is to have to have the MSN Messenger installed on both computers.

To ask for remote assistant do the following:

1. Click the Start button.

2. Select All Programs.

3. Select Remote Assistant.

4. The Help and Support Center window will launch (Figure 6.22) showing you two options. You can send an invitation to people using Windows Messenger or send an invitation through e-mail.

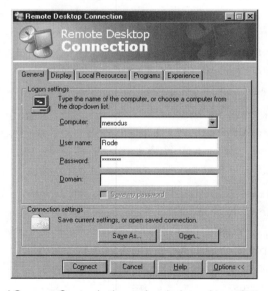

Figure 6.22 *Help and Support Center is the main window where you are able to request assistance from your contacts using the Windows Messenger. You can also send an invitation by e-mail.*

The MSN Messenger allows you to view the online status of people you have entered into your MSN Messenger contact (buddy) list. If you send the invitation using the MSN Messenger to a user that is online, it will be received immediately. As soon as your invitation is accepted the Remote Assistant program will start.

To install the MSN Messenger, visit *http://messenger.msn.com/*.

Summary

Networks are more than printer-sharing devices or gateways to the Internet. Your home network allows you to share resources, files, and even your entire desktop with others on your network or on the Internet. Because of this, be careful when sharing resources—make sure that they are adequately protected. Hackers are constantly in search of unprotected shared resources.

There are software programs such as Symantec's PC Anywhere that has provided remote desktop access for many years. These features are now being built right into the operating system, giving your home network an incredible amount of power and flexibility.

Sharing
the Internet

7

Many homes now have more than one computer in the house. This statistic is growing exponentially. These homes, some of them equipped with broadband (high-bandwidth), "always on" connections, will want each computer in the home connected to the single, dedicated connection. This chapter discusses one of the most popular reasons for creating a home network—allowing more than one PC to access the Internet at the same time using the same Internet connection.

One of the challenges of the dedicated home Internet connection is usually the single IP address allotted to the home. In the case of cable modem connections, this limitation is pretty much written in stone. Other dedicated connection types, such as DSL business connections, are allowed more than one IP address.

Here is the challenge:

• Each computer must have a unique IP address.

• Each computer connected to the Internet must have an IP address allotted (routed) by the ISP (Internet Service Provider).

• Local IP addresses cannot be used to route traffic over the Internet. Therefore there must be a way to route local traffic destined to the Internet through a single IP address.

Figure 7.1 shows a typical scenario in which a home has two computers connected to a network hub. The cable or DSL modem also connects to the network hub. The modem then connects to the ISP—shown as a cloud in Figure 7.1.

To be connected to the Internet, your network must be connected by at least one IP address given to you by your ISP. Every computer on your home network can connect to the Internet using that single IP address, using either a *router* or a *proxy server*.

Routers

Routers, sometimes known as gateways, are software or hardware devices that connect two networks. They "route" traffic between the two networks. When you connect your home network to the Internet, this is exactly what you are doing—connecting two networks, your network and the Internet.

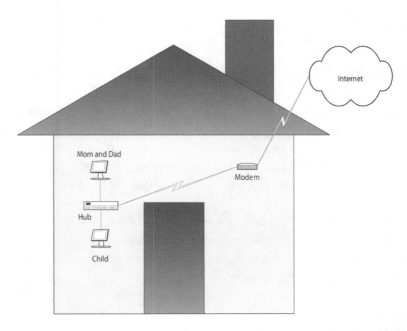

Figure 7.1 *More than one computer can be connected to the Internet over a home network.*

There are two ways traffic can be routed to your network by your ISP. One way is to give you as many IP addresses as you have computers on your network. You then configure each router to send traffic bound for these computers to the appropriate computer on your network. The other possibility is to grant you one IP address. This IP address is used by the cable or DSL modem and each computer on your network uses a special, non-Internet IP address. The cable or DSL modem then acts like a router and sends traffic to the correct computer within your network.

Most homes will probably use only a single IP address. Being assigned multiple IP addresses can be very expensive and usually requires a business Internet account. Therefore, your network will most likely be doing its own routing and sharing a single Internet-ready IP address.

One very popular type of router is the Linksys Etherfast Cable/DSL router with a four-port switch. This device can be used instead of a network hub to interconnect your local network. This will save you a little money. If you are using a wireless network, you would plug your wireless base into this router.

The LinkSys router allows you to have up to 253 users, which is more than enough to support most families and guests.

How Routers Work

Each router has its own IP address. When you are connecting your network to the Internet with a single IP address given to you by your ISP, this becomes the IP address of the router. Any other computers on your network are given a special IP address reserved specifically for LANs and not the Internet.

The IP address used for your local machines depends on the size of your network. The size of your network (number of computers connected) determines the *class* of the network.

There are three primary classes of networks designated A, B, and C. There is actually a Class D block of IP addresses for multicasting, a means of broadcasting data onto a network without forming a peer-to-peer connection. There is also a Class E block of addresses reserved for experiments.

A Class A network is reserved for the major Internet trunk providers. These are companies that provide services to the major ISPs. There are 127 possible Class A networks with a total of 16,777,214 possible computers on each network. The reserved IP addresses for a Class A network begin with 10, and all the other numbers in each of the four groups range from 0 to 255 (10.xxx.xxx.xxx).

A Class B network is the one most often used by large ISPs. There are a total of 16,382 possible Class B networks each capable of supporting 65,534 computers. Class B networks have two reserved ranges beginning with 172 and 16 or 172 and 31 respectively (172.16.x.x, 172.31.x.x).

Class C networks are the most common networks, supporting a total of 256 computers for each network. On the Internet there are a total of 4,194,304 possible Class C networks. However, because the IP address range used locally on your local network will not be visible on the Internet, you can use any IP address range you want. A router on your local network will be situated between the Internet and the computers on your local network. It is a recommended standard that you use the reserved address range for a Class C network 192.168.x.x, with each x having a number that ranges between 0 and 255. It is this address range you will use for your home network (see Figure 7.2).

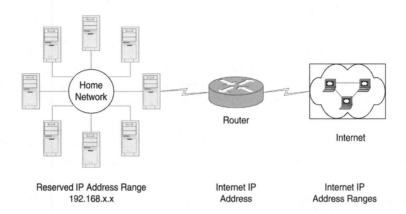

Reserved IP Address Range
192.168.x.x

Internet IP
Address

Internet IP
Address Ranges

Figure 7.2 *Your router has an Internet IP address; your local computers do not.*

Note: Using the reserved IP address range on your home network is not a requirement but a good recommendation to follow. In the future, you may need technical
support and using IP addresses outside of this range may confuse support personnel.

When your computer sends information to the Internet, it is sent out with
the IP address of the router. When information returns from the Internet
bound for your computer, the router sends the information to your computer.
It knows where to send information based on an internal configuration table
maintained by the router.

When you configure Internet Connection Sharing on your Windows computer, this computer begins acting as a router. See the Internet Connection
Sharing section later in this chapter for more information.

The configuration table contains not only the local IP address of your computer, but also a *physical address*. A computer's IP address can change each time
it connects to a network. The one thing that does not change is a special code
hard-coded into the computer's NIC. This code is known as the MAC (Media
Access Control) address. The router makes note of the MAC address and stores
it in its configuration table.

You will never have a reason to know the MAC address of your computer. If
you are curious anyway, you can run the WINIPCFG utility by clicking Start,

choosing Run, typing WINIPCFG, and hitting the Enter key. This utility will display a number of useful bits of information about your computer's network configuration.

Note: It is possible for a computer to have more than one network card installed. In this case, the computer can have more than one physical address. Having more than one network card allows a single computer to communicate on more than one network at the same time.

The router on your network uses the *Address Resolution Protocol* (ARP) to discover and maintain its list of physical addresses. That is all well and good, but how does the router know where to send incoming information meant for your computer? *Network Address Translation* (NAT) works like a network receptionist. The following is a scenario demonstrating communication with NAT.

When computer A sends a request to the Internet, it checks in with NAT and lets NAT know that it is expecting an answer. When the expected answer arrives, the router or other NAT-enabled device knows where to send the information. For example, imagine computer A is sitting on a home network with two other computers. It sends a request to *http://www.yahoo.com*, which at the moment happens to be IP address 216.115.102.78. The NAT software makes note of the fact that computer A just communicated with that IP address and sent a GET request. When the response comes from 216.115.102.78 to computer A's request, NAT routes the response to computer A.

The good thing about NAT and ARP is that you do not have to worry about them. They do their tasks completely unattended and without your assistance. The information about them was included because sometimes it helps to understand some of the "magic" in the black boxes we hook together. With some understanding of the technology, configuring your network makes more sense, and the job becomes simpler and more interesting.

DHCP Servers

As mentioned in Chapter 5, DHCP is a software program that manages a block of IP addresses. A DHCP server is configured with a block of IP addresses. When a computer connects to the Internet and requests an IP address, the DHCP server program gives the computer an IP address from its list.

On a home network, in which you will probably have less than ten IP addresses, this is probably not an issue. But imagine the plight of the ISP. Let us say they are given 10,000 IP addresses. If each customer were given an IP address, that would be 10,000 customers, and not one more. A DHCP server allows the ISP to offer the IP addresses on a "time-share" basis. It lets the ISP serve 100,000 customers intermittently connected, instead of only 10,000.

When using a DHCP service, you may not be given the same IP address each time your network connects. The IP address you are provided by a DHCP server is known as a dynamic IP address. When you are given an IP address that remains the same, it is known as a static IP address. Be aware that when using DHCP, your dynamic IP address may change occasionally. Even dedicated connections disconnect at times, usually due to problems on the network.

Using a DHCP Server at Home

Just as an ISP can use a DHCP server to conserve the use of their allotted IP addresses, so can you. You can set up your own DHCP server to hand out the IP addresses you are allotted. If you are only given a single IP address, you should consider using a router and/or proxy server instead. Refer to the Proxy Servers section later in this chapter for more information.

If you decide to spend some extra money, you can have more than one IP address for your network. If you are given five IP addresses and you have seven computers, not all of the computers will be able to connect to the Internet at the same time. You can use a DHCP server to hand out the available IP addresses on a first-come, first-served basis. Computers that log on to the network after all of the Internet IP addresses have been handed out can be given a local IP address so that the computer can still take advantage of local network resources and be able to communicate with the other computers on your home network.

Setting up a DHCP Server

If you already have an operating system that has a DHCP server installed, such as Windows 2000 server, you can start providing DHCP services by configuring the server. The steps to configure the DHCP server for Windows 2000 specifically are included, but you will find that all DHCP servers have the same basic configuration. Follow these steps to configure DHCP on Windows 2000:

1. Launch the DHCP management interface by selecting DHCP from Administrative Tools in the Windows 2000 Start menu. This will launch the interface shown in Figure 7.3.

2. Configure the pool of available IP addresses by right-clicking on the Scope folder, as shown in Figure 7.3. Select Properties from the popup menu.

3. Set the start and end IP addresses in the Server Scope Properties window shown in Figure 7.4 by entering them in the labeled fields.

4. Set any limitations on the amount of time you want someone to be able to continue using an IP address before resetting the connection. This setting is what often causes people to lose connection to their ISP. The ISP can control the turnover of people connected to their network by setting this value to a low duration.

5. Optionally set the name and description of this configuration by entering a name and description in the labeled fields.

The DNS Tab allows you to configure your DHCP server so that it updates a DNS server automatically when a computer connects and retrieves an IP address. This is particularly important if another computer needs to contact your computer using its FQDN. Your DNS server will be able to resolve the FQDN to the IP address issued by the DHCP server.

The Advanced tab allows you to set the properties of the DHCP server so that it will accept requests from DHCP clients and/or *bootp* clients. Bootp is a protocol used by diskless workstations to dynamically discover their IP address.

You can reserve an IP address for a particular computer. There are some software programs that require that the computer always have the same IP address. To reserve an IP address using the Windows 2000 DHCP Server, click New Reservation from the Action menu.

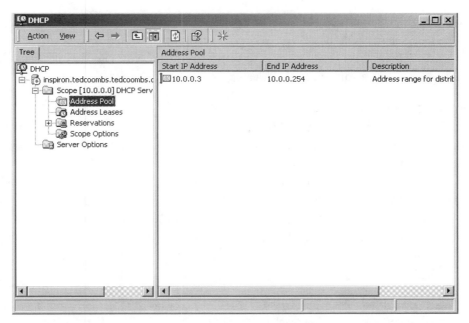

Figure 7.3 *The Windows 2000 DHCP configuration interface gives you access to server properties.*

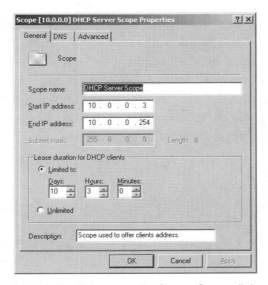

Figure 7.4 *Set start and end IP addresses in the Server Scope dialog.*

It is useful to exclude the use of certain IP addresses that may already be assigned to services such as Web servers. By defining IP addresses to exclude, you do not allow the DHCP server to hand them out.You can define an exclusion range within a range of IP addresses to reserve more than one address.

Hardware DHCP Devices

DHCP servers are often embedded in devices other than your computer. For example, many routers and broadband modems have DHCP servers built in. Many of the more popular networking brands such as Linksys, D–Link, and Netgear manufacture products with embedded DHCP server capability.

Many hardware DHCP servers come preconfigured. For example, the Netgear Cable/DSL Firewall Router comes preconfigured so that the internal DHCP server assigns local IP addresses in the range of 192.168.0.2 to 192.168.0.31, a gateway address of 192.168.0.1, and a subnet mask of 255.255.255.0.

Warning! If you have purchased a piece of hardware that has an embedded DHCP server, you must first disable any other software DHCP servers running on your network before plugging the new hardware into your network.

You can manage the DHCP settings by logging into your system, usually with a Web browser. Point your Web browser to the IP address assigned to the gateway—in many cases this address will be *http://192.168.0.1.* Your Web browser will most likely launch an administrative software interface that allows you to modify many of the network settings, and in particular, the DHCP settings of your router or hardware device with embedded DHCP server functionality.

You should find that configuring the DHCP server on your hardware device is nearly identical to the software configuration described in the previous section of this chapter.

Wireless DHCP Service

Mobile DHCP Service, a software program you can download from the Internet, enhances existing DHCP service by sensing your computer's interrupted connection to the wireless network.Your wireless computer or mobile device then attempts to reconnect to the network, requesting a new IP address from the DHCP server.

This feature allows mobile devices to move from network to network, connecting with a new IP address on each network. This ability to roam from network to network will allow you to move a wireless device from your home network to other wireless networks in places such as coffee shops that now allow you to connect to the Internet over their wireless networks.

You can download the software from

http://shareit1.element5.com/programs.html?productid=152329.

Proxy Servers and Firewalls

A proxy server is not the same thing as a firewall. Sometimes the abilities of both come bundled in the same software program.

Proxy Servers

A proxy server is a computer running special proxy-server software used to protect and speed up network traffic by acting as a "middle man" in the connection so that no computers outside the network can communicate directly with computers on the local network. Protocol data is handed off between the two networks through the proxy server.

Note: Some proxy servers use a special communications protocol known as SOCKS.

A computer acting as a proxy server is normally connected directly to the broadband network and acts as a gateway to other computers on the network, providing proxy services for servers running on other machines on the network. This means, for example, that if you are running a Web server on your network, it is not necessary to have the Web server on the machine connected directly to the broadband network. The proxy server can "fetch" the Web page from the Web server on your network and deliver it to the client. Because the proxy server can remember these pages, keeping them in a special area of memory called a cache, the proxy server can deliver them over and over again without bothering the Web server. This reduces network traffic and speeds up network services.

Proxy server programs can also act as routers, allowing you to preserve IP address usage in the same way as a hardware or software router program. The only required Internet IP address is the one used by the proxy server computer directly connected to the network. Because of this, your proxy server machine will need two NICs, one to connect to the broadband network and one to connect to your local LAN. When you configure the network cards, you will assign the local IP address block to the network card servicing the local LAN and the single Internet IP address to the network card servicing the broadband connection. Assign these IP addresses in the network settings for your computer.

Proxy servers can act like firewalls. Firewall software listens to incoming requests from the Internet and selectively blocks traffic, usually by port number. Firewalls also have the ability to block requests from certain IP addresses or domains. For example, if your network is continuously bombarded or hacked from a specific IP address, you can place that address on a "blacklist" that will tell the firewall software to just ignore any requests from that IP address

An example of a proxy server with firewall capabilities is WinRoute Pro, which can be downloaded at the following URL:

http://serverwatch.internet.com/proxyserver-winroute.html

Firewalls

A firewall is a piece of equipment or software program that serves one purpose: to protect one network from another. Of course networks by themselves rarely have a nefarious purpose or intent. It is the people who use them that have bad intentions. Unfortunately, the malicious code unleashed by hackers over time has literally infected networks to the point where the networks themselves are "sick" and it is necessary to protect one network from another.

Firewall Software

Firewalls incorporate the functionality of the NAT router. Beyond simply forwarding packets, firewalls are normally equipped with an array of security features. Most of these features are designed to identify and stop intruders. When intruders are detected, the firewall can

- Log the incident
- Notify an administrator
- Sound an alarm
- Take evasive action by denying access

Some firewall software will even begin detection procedures to hunt down and identify the intruder.

One of the ways firewalls differ from simple routers is packet filtering. Packet filters accept or reject packets based on a set of rules.

There are two levels of packet filtering, *dynamic packet inspection* and *stateful packet inspection*. Dynamic packet inspection opens and closes "doors" or ports on an as-needed basis. A more sophisticated means of packet filtering is the stateful packet inspection. Stateful packet inspection inspects incoming packets at the application layer and analyzes them with some level of intelligence about previous packets received in this connection and about the protocol being used in the connection. The stateful packet inspector routine can detect errors in the protocol which may be identified as means to insert malicious code onto the network.

Firewall Hardware

Some equipment such as broadband routers have firewalls built right into them. This is probably all you will need for your home network. Industrial-strength networks normally use a computer as the hardware firewall. This computer normally has an operating system with no frills installed. This eliminates any ability for a hacker to exploit extraneous applications. Sacrificing a computer on your network is probably overkill for your home network. All you really need is a broadband router. The firewall built into many broadband routers will be able to

- Filter access to the Internet, based on IP address or MAC address.
- Open or close a range of port numbers.
- Set certain IP addresses to pass through the firewall.
- Remotely configure your router from any Web browser in the world if you desire. This is an optional feature and should probably not be left enabled for obvious reasons.

Remember that the security provided by a firewall does not prevent you or other people using your home network from downloading malicious code or viruses. Good virus protection software in addition to a firewall is strongly recommended. These two types of security will protect your network from most types of intrusion or damage.

ICS (Internet Connection Sharing)

ICS is a NAT-based routing program. Running this on a computer connected to your home network allows more than one computer to share a single IP address. The beauty of ICS is that you can use this service with both dial-up and broadband services. Many of the routing solutions discussed so far are best used only with dedicated broadband solutions.

 Warning! Because ICS requires two network adapters—either physical or software dial-up adapters—this program will not work with one-way (unidirectional services) such as DirecPC.

Installing ICS on Windows 98 or Me

To install ICS in Windows 98 or Me, you will need to first install the ICS software. Windows 2000 and XP come with ICS preinstalled.

Before installing ICS on a network in which computers use DHCP to obtain an IP address, shut down these computers on your network. This way the computers will be sure to obtain an IP address from the ICS DHCP server, rather than the DHCP server your computer used previously.

ICS requires that the computer on which it is installed have two NICs installed. This is because this computer will serve as a bridge between the broadband connection and the LAN. You will need to make sure that the NIC is supported by your cable or DSL modem.

To get started, you will need to start the Internet Connection Sharing Wizard (Figure 7.5).

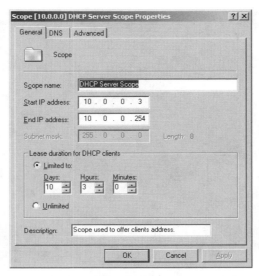

Figure 7.5 *Start the Internet Sharing Wizard and click Next to continue.*

1. In the Control Panel, select Add/Remove Programs.

2. Click the Windows Setup tab.

3. Find the Internet Tools icon and double-click on it.

4. Check the Internet Connection Sharing box.

5. Click OK.

This will cause the ICS program to install. Once it has been installed, the Internet Sharing Wizard will automatically launch.

Select the type of connection your network will use by clicking the appropriate radio button. Figure 7.6 shows the selection for broadband access. Click the Next button when you are ready to continue to the next step.

This next step is critical. The list that appears should contain the description of at least two NICs. You must select the one that is connected to the Internet and not the NIC that connects to your home network. If you select incorrectly, your installation will not work. Click the Next button to continue onto the next step.

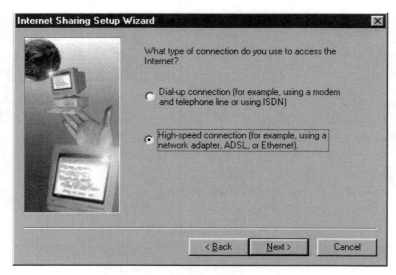

Figure 7.6 *Set the connection type by clicking either radio button.*

You can skip the creation of a Client Configuration Disk. Just click the Next button to continue to the next page, where you will click the Finish button. Your computer will then reboot to finish the installation.

Installing ICS on Windows 2000

As in the installation above, your computer will need two NICs for ICS to work. To install ICS on Windows 2000, follow these steps:

1. Configure your dial-up networking profile or install your broadband connection.
2. Install the second network card for your home network. Set up the properties for your home network.
3. Edit the properties of the NIC that is connected to your broadband connection or edit your dial-up adapter properties.
4. Click the Sharing tab.
5. Check the Enable Shared Access for this connection box to set your computer to use ICS. If you are configuring a dial-up adapter, you will also need to check the Enable on–demand dialing box so that your computer will dial when a network client requests Internet access.

Summary

Chances are good that your home network will need to share a single IP address for Internet access. There are several ways of configuring your network to use this IP address. One way, using a router, is probably the simplest and most secure. Routers normally have firewall software embedded in them. The alternative is to use a computer on your network as a gateway, installing two network cards in the same computer and using ICS software. The information in this chapter helped you understand the idea of local versus Internet IP addresses and how to configure routers, firewalls, and Internet connection sharing software. Chapter 8 will describe how to manage different aspects of your home network.

Managing Your Home Network 8

Once installed, your home network should provide years of trouble-free service. There are no moving parts, so in theory there is nothing to wear out. There are no serviceable parts in a network. Therefore, unless your network hardware actually breaks, there is no need to replace it.

Managing a home network has more to do with managing the computers attached to the network, using features of the network. The two most important network management tasks are protecting your network from hackers and malicious code, and maintaining the network with backups.

Training

Networks are generally underutilized because people do not know how to use them to their fullest capacity. Once you have installed a network in your home, it is a great idea to train everyone in your household how to use its features.

Here are some topics you will want to cover:

• How to install and use printers shared over a network
• How to share and stop sharing folders on your hard drive
• How to set up security when sharing folders
• How to use a shared folder
• How to set up a network drive

You may also want to explain how bandwidth works. It is good to know why downloads from the Internet may take a long time. Problems arise when Sue is downloading MP3 files, Danny is downloading a feature-length film, mom is video conferencing, and dad cannot figure out why it is taking ten minutes for his chicken recipe page to download.

Explaining why it is good to organize your hard drive to make backups easier is always helpful. This topic is explained further in this chapter.

Protecting your Network

You should familiarize yourself with some basic concepts that will allow you to understand and protect your network from people who wish to harm you by gaining unauthorized access to your home network.

The most important thing to understand is how software communicates with other software over a network. There are two protocols (languages used by software to communicate): TCP (Transmission Control Protocol) and UDP (User Datagram Protocol). These two protocols enable two-way communication between software programs over a network.

You already know that your computer has an IP address. This identifies your computer. Each application that is running on your computer that intends to communicate with another program over a network is assigned a special number, called a port. This enables information headed to a specific IP address to be routed to the correct program. Normally, one program will listen for traffic directed to a specific port number, and then respond when contacted. This type of listening application is normally called a server, while the program that contacts a server is known as a client. Some common port numbers used by Internet applications are 80 for the World Wide Web, and 25 or 110 for e-mail.

Hackers will often use a software program known as a port scanner. This program points at your IP address and then tries to contact software on a range of port numbers. Certain types of virus programs, such as Trojan horses (explained later in this chapter) will listen for specific port numbers. When the port scanner finds a Trojan program, placed there previously by the same or a different hacker, the person using the port scanner can gain access to your computer, possibly watching everything you type, including your password or credit card numbers.

Managing Disk Space

When you share a folder or disk as a network resource, you are inviting others to use that disk. If you allow others on your network to write information to that disk, you should be careful to manage your available disk space carefully.

 Note: Using Windows Explorer, you can easily view the available disk space by clicking on the name of the hard drive.

Allowing others to store information on your hard drive can quickly become unmanageable if they have no concept of how much information they are storing. You can manage this by creating directories specifically for the purpose of allowing remote file storage. Review the available hard disk space regularly. If you notice that the available space suddenly decreases, you can review the contents of the shared folders to see where the disk storage is being used.

Managing Security

Some of the features that make networks useful also make them security risks. Sharing network resources such as folders and hard drives, unless carefully managed, can cause parts of your hard drive to be shared with the general public over the Internet. See Chapter 6 for more information about setting security on shared resources.

You may wonder why it is so important to protect your computer. After all, you may not know anyone who would want to break into your computer. What you must remember is that you may use your computer for many private things, such as banking, accounting, and e-mail correspondence. Your personal information and that of your family should remain private.

Often times, people who gain access to your computer do so, not with the intent of gaining access to your private information, but to use your computer as a platform from which to launch attacks on other computers. They may use your e-mail address to send viruses, or spam (unsolicited e-mail) to hundreds, thousands, or tens of thousands of people on the Internet. Imagine all the hate mail you will get, in addition to bounced mail notifications (the e-mail from mail servers notifying you of an invalid e-mail address). It is guaranteed that if this happens, you will be miserable.

Threats to Security

Trojans, worms, hackers, and viruses sound like the subjects of a reality TV show. Hackers are individuals who use their knowledge of computers to gain unauthorized access to computer systems. Often hackers will use programs planted on your computer called Trojans (or Trojan horse programs) to surreptitiously access a computer. Hackers sometimes try to gain access just for the thrill of defeating your computer's security. Oftentimes the goal is far worse, such as theft of your private or financial information stored on your computer.

In addition to hackers trying to gain access to your computer, you also face the dangers of small programs written by programmers that attempt to damage your computer. Virus programs, as they are known, all have one thing in common—they attempt to spread themselves, usually using your e-mail program. Whether they do any further damage to your computer once installed depends on the type of virus.

Hackers

There are several definitions of the word *hacker.* The one you should be concerned about is the one that describes hackers as people who try to gain surreptitious access to computer systems for illegal purposes.

Hackers are not always technogeeks that spend their lives programming or writing viruses. In fact, the most notorious hacker of this day and age is Kevin Mitnick. Mitnick used a principle known as social engineering. He would call people on the phone and convince them that he was someone else, and would then convince them to give him access to computer systems, phone systems, or any other kind of system to which he wanted access.

For this reason, it is important to protect your network from more than viruses and Trojans. Be careful when giving information through the Internet. There have been several very convincing hoaxes in which very convincing software programs have asked for private information such as credit card numbers, passwords, social security numbers and more.

Hackers generally use more than social engineering. They look for vulnerabilities in your network to gain entry. One simple trick is to try and guess your password. There are programs that will try most of the commonly used passwords first.

In addition to hacking passwords, there are several vulnerabilities in Web browser and instant messaging software that allows the hacker to gain entry. The hacker, by sending too much data or the wrong type of data, causes the program to malfunction and this may allow him or her access to your computers. This kind of attack is known as a *buffer overflow.* It is a complex way of exploiting the weaknesses of network software. If you would like to know more about buffer overflows you can read The Tao of Windows Buffer Overflow: *http://www.cultdeadcow.com/cDc_files/cDc-351/*.

Another annoying practice, not necessarily done by hackers, is something known as a denial-of-service attack. This type of attack usually targets Web servers. A malicious requestor makes so many requests of the Web server that the server software and machine can no longer keep up with the requests, and is unable to deliver Web pages to legitimate requests.

Viruses

Everyone has heard of computer viruses. Dangerous viruses are covered in news headlines several times a year. What you do not hear in the news is that the viruses you hear about once in the news continue damaging computers all over the world, seven days a week, twenty-four hours a day. Protecting yourself from these malicious programs is one of the most important efforts you can make. There are two basic classes of viruses.

- Virus programs that perform some malicious task and then try to replicate themselves.
- Trojans that secretly allow a user to access your computer remotely.

Viruses are undesirable computer programs that you receive surreptitiously on your computer. The primary function of a virus is to make copies of itself and attempt to infect another computer. The secondary function of a virus program varies depending on how it is written.

On one end of the scale, a virus may simply display a harmless message, "tagging" your computer. This is tantamount to spray painting "Kilgore was here." on your computer. The virus is annoying, but the severity of the threat to your computer is very low.

High-threat viruses can wreak severe damage to your computer software. These malicious programs may alter or erase programs that allow your computer to continue to operate or reboot. Viruses may delete important data and leave you without the ability to retrieve the deleted information.

Virus Infection

Your computer can become infected with a virus in many different ways. All infection mechanisms have one thing in common—your computer must accept, knowingly or unknowingly, the transfer of data into the computer. This data can be in the form of a Web page, word-processing document, electronic photo, software program, or e-mail. Moving data into your computer, whether it is from a floppy disk, CD-ROM, DVD-ROM, over the local network, or downloaded from the Internet, always poses a risk.

There have been occurrences in which commercial software has been unwittingly infected with a virus. In these cases, even buying software in a shrink-wrapped box has spread viruses.

Protecting yourself from viruses is extremely important. It is highly recommended that you use one of the premier virus protection software programs. There are two that stand above the others, Norton Antivirus (*http://www.symantec.com/*) and McAfee (*http://www.mcafee.com/*).

Trojans

Trojans are a type of malicious computer program named after the Greek Trojan horse story, in which soldiers hid within a large wooden horse that was offered to the enemy as a gift. A Trojan program hides on your hard drive like a virus, but does not make copies of itself. Trojans are often used to provide remote control of your computer.

Trojans are similar to other malicious virus programs. Some Trojans propagate as a virus, while others are intentionally deposited by a hacker. The Trojan program, in that case, does not concern itself with sending itself to others.

One of the best ways to protect yourself from Trojans is to use a software program designed specifically for Trojans. The Lockdown Trojan protection software does a good job (*http://www.lockdowncorp.com/*).

Worms

Worms are a type of computer virus. These programs replicate—making copies of themselves both within a single computer and over a network. Worms have been shown to be some of the most destructive of all the computer viruses. The Nimda virus and Code Red are both worms.

Preventing Losses

Unfortunately, the preceding section only scratches the surface when it comes to the kinds of threats people conceive of every single day. The best way to protect your network of computers is to educate yourself about the most current threats. Try to evaluate the warnings sent by your friends. Most of these virus warnings are hoaxes. You can access the most current virus information from Symantec.com, home of the Norton antivirus program, or from McAffee.com, home of the McAffee virus protection program.

In addition to knowing about the latest threats, you can take action to protect your network by installing a firewall. Firewalls are either software programs or hardware devices that sit between your computer and the Internet and provide a high level of security (see Chapter 7, Proxy Servers and Firewalls).

There is no absolute protection against hackers and viruses. Therefore, your best defense is a good backup. When all else goes wrong, if you have faithfully backed up the data on your computer, you can restore any data you may have lost to malicious code.

Firewalls

In the early days of the Internet, hackers began attacking the relatively insecure UNIX computers that were primarily used to access and provide services over the Internet. As fast as programmers could patch a security hole, another would be exploited. UNIX was like Swiss cheese to a hacker. There was only one thing that could put an instant stop to the havoc being wreaked by hackers—a firewall.

The first firewalls were all computers designed to sit between a network and the Internet. The firewall computer would run no software that could be hacked and would provide only one service—to act as a gatekeeper to the software services on the network it was guarding.

The computers behind the firewall could remain relatively open and insecure, without worry that hackers could gain entry from the Internet. Firewalls act as proxies for the software that still need access to the Internet.

As we mentioned earlier in this chapter, software communicates using specific port numbers to identify the application to which data sent across a network should be routed. Firewalls block data traffic to your network by blocking all but a few ports. By default, firewall software and hardware will not block access to ports 80, 25, and 110—the well-known WWW and e-mail ports. You can then further configure your firewall to allow traffic on other ports as they become necessary. For example, you might allow traffic on ports to allow the use of instant-message programs such as ICQ or AOL Instant Messenger.

Which ports a program uses to communicate through are not always readily apparent. You sometimes have to be a sleuth to find this information. Most software companies will publish this information somewhere because they are accustomed to the requirement of communicating through firewalls.

Firewalls will not make your network impregnable. They will, however, eliminate the ability of most hackers to gain unauthorized access to computers on your network.

Network Backups

No amount of effort can protect the computers on your network from every type of malicious damage or simple hardware failure. There is only one safety net that you can create and that is a backup system for the information on your computers. We cannot stress enough how important it is to back up your critical data. Networks make backing up data much easier. Hard drives can be shared over the network, allowing backup hardware and software the ability to back up more than one computer from a single location.

The Plan

It is not necessary to back up your entire hard drive. Backing up everything takes a lot of time, consumes backup media such as tapes or CDs, and is usually unnecessary. Most of the information stored on your hard drive is saved there when you install software programs. In the event that you lose data, either through attack by a virus or by hardware failure, chances are good that you can reinstall all or most of the software from the media on which it was originally stored. For example, your operating system is probably available on a CD-ROM.

Organize your hard disk so that your saved documents are all within the same directory hierarchy. In other words, if you have a folder named My Documents, create subfolders for other types of documents you normally work with, such as word-processing files, spreadsheet files, pictures, and graphics. Sharing the My Documents folder will allow the computer running the backup program to back up this directory only, rather than sharing and backing up many directories. For more information on sharing folders and Network Neighborhood see Chapter 6, Network Sharing.

The Hardware

There are several options for backing up your computer system. Options are recommended in this section based on reliability, simplicity, and cost. No matter which option you choose, make certain that you somehow automate the task of network backup. Everyone always begins with the best of intentions, and eventually the backup chore gets set aside for more pressing issues, until of course, the whole system comes crashing down and you realize the latest backup was six months ago.

Tape Drives

There are a number of different tape backup systems on the market. Most of them are pretty reliable and come with powerful software that allows you to automate your backups. Magnetic tape normally comes in a small cartridge, some even as small as microcassettes. Tape backup is fairly inexpensive, simple to perform, and moderately fast. Also, most tape systems can support tapes with multigigabyte storage capacity.

There are challenges with tape, however. First, if your computer crashes, chances are good that you do not have the tape backup software installed on the new hard drive to retrieve the backup from tape. Most tape drive systems require special software to retrieve the information from the tape. Second, it is difficult to restore part of a backup, meaning that it is possible that you could overwrite newer files with older versions. Third, you can not use tape like you would a hard drive or CD-ROM because tapes are not random access. Lastly, magnetic tape is prone to failure (eaten by the machine) or demagnetized due to improper handling.

Writeable CD-ROM

CDROMs are an excellent way to deliver software. Writeable and rewriteable CD-ROMS have nearly replaced floppy disks for saving moderate amounts of data at home. With a storage capacity of around 500 MB, CD-ROM burners or CD Writers as they are called, can write significantly more data than the older floppy disk (1.2 MB).

CD-ROMs have a number of advantages over other media. They are fairly indestructible and they can be accessed like any other disk so there is no need to restore, as in tape backup systems. The major disadvantage of CD-ROMs is also one of its advantages—storage space. Though 500 MB is a lot of storage compared to disks, with hard drives surpassing 100 GB (100,000 MB) it would take a large number of CD-ROMs to save that amount of data. Of course, as we said previously, most of the data will be application programs (which do not require backup), and one or two CD-ROMs may be sufficient to back up your critical data.

Writeable DVD-ROM

Writeable DVD-ROM is more expensive than writeable CD-ROM, but with a storage capacity of 4.7 GB, the problem of storage space is considerably reduced. Note that it would still take just over twenty DVD-ROMs to back up a 100 GB hard drive, however.

Jaz and Zip Cartridges

A once popular alternative to tape (before writeable CD-ROMs) were special floppy cartridges called Zip disks and Jaz disks. These are products of Iomega (*www.iomega.com*). Iomega's cartridge system was innovative in that it allowed random access to large amounts of data in removable cartridges, thereby overcoming one of the major disadvantages of tape systems. However, times have changed along with the abilities and costs of newer technologies. The technology and cost of Jaz and Zip drives make these a poor option. The Jaz drive can store up to 2 GB, but at a cost of over $120 per cartridge on top of the cost of the Jaz drive.

Third-Party Internet Backup

Internet backup services provide you the ability to move your important data to an offsite location, saving it from theft, fire, damage, or other types of loss. The advantages to an Internet backup service is that you do not have to concern yourself with the size of the backup media, or purchase new media. Backup services will provide you the backup storage space to fit your need.

Because the storage is away from your home, you can rest assured that your data is completely safe. Of course, it is only completely safe as long as the service provider remains in business. In fact, most backup services will encrypt your information before it leaves your computer so that your information resides at their location in an encrypted and secure form. This will protect it from hackers.

You can upload your files to a hard drive over the Internet and have access to those files from anywhere you may happen to be on the Internet. You may even find services that are ad-sponsored and free.

The downsides to this type of service are that it requires that you have an Internet connection and that your computer is capable of connecting to the Internet. You must also pay a continual storage fee instead of a one-time fee to pay for backup hardware and media. If, for some reason, you cannot pay the fee, you can say goodbye to your data.

 Warning! Free services tend to be pretty volatile, and you never know when they might go out of business, taking your data with them.

Backup Hard Drive

Perhaps the simplest, and most cost effective means of backing up data is to purchase an additional hard drive, install it, and copy your data to it.

Hard drives, although not cheap, usually cost the same or less than tape backup systems, and considerably less than DVD-ROM burners. Hard drives can be copied, and even stored somewhere else, such as a safe deposit box, if you are concerned about your data being lost to fire, theft, or other reasons beyond your control. Of course, even a safe deposit box is no guarantee of complete safety.

Aside from cost, the advantage of having a complete backup copy of your hard drive is that should your current drive fail, you can drop in the backup media and pick up where you left off. It is easiest to leave the hard drive installed in the computer to make regular backups easier. If you are concerned about your backup hard drive failing, consider leaving it installed in your computer, opening the case, and removing the power plug from the drive. Anything with a moving part has a tendency to fail. You can feel fairly certain that the hard drive will work again when power is reapplied. Remember to turn the power off to your computer before removing or applying power to your drive.

Hot Swappable Drive

There is another more convenient, and slightly more expensive, hard-drive solution called a hot-swappable hard drive. Plug this external hard drive into your computer through a USB or Firewire port while the computer is running and you will have access to the hard drive for backup or data storage requirements.

The drives are lightweight and portable, which makes them very convenient. You do not have to bother with opening your computer to install anything. No tools are required, just plug it in and start using the drive. You can even use the same hot-swappable hard drive in more than one computer.

The down side to drives, hot swappable or installed, is that the machine and media are a single unit. Should you need additional storage instead of buying more media, you must buy an additional unit.

Summary

Installing a home network is only the first step. Once it is up and running and configured correctly, the next job is managing the network. Training everyone to use all the features of the network will make your lives easier and maximize your investment in a home network. Also, managing the day-to-day details of things like security and disk space will keep things running smoothly.

Unfortunately, we do not live in a perfect world and leaving your network unprotected from viruses and hackers will only bring you eventual grief. There are tens of thousands of viruses, worms, and Trojans just waiting to attack the computers on your network. No security is perfectly failsafe but making your best attempt at protecting your network from outside attack will reduce the risk of losing all or some of the data on your computer permanently. A considerable loss would cause you hours, if not days, of work restoring your computer to an operational state.

Managing your home network is not a burden, and will not require much your time. It will only require a minimal amount of attention to avoid disasters that will certainly take a great deal of your time to recover.

Troubleshooting the Network

9

Networking has not quite reached the point where "it just works." Though many networking tools have made networking much simpler, even to the point of being plug-and-play, there is still a large possibility that your network may not work the first time or that it may stop working at some point. The information you learned in this book for setting up a network will also provide you with an excellent foundation for troubleshooting a network that is not functioning properly.

You will know when your network is malfunctioning when one or more of the computers on the network fail in some way to communicate with other computers on the network. Sometimes network failures are "all or nothing." Sometimes only one expected behavior, such as print and file sharing, fail to operate as expected.

This chapter will explain some of the tools and procedures available for finding and correcting network problems. There are no home-networking problems that are unsolvable, and solving them does not require a network engineer. The best tool you can have in your network troubleshooting arsenal is patience.

Unlike many software applications, such as word processors and Web browsers, network applications run invisibly in the background. When they are misconfigured, they may not operate and will not give you an error message or clue as to why they are failing. For this reason, creating a structured approach to network troubleshooting is imperative.

Is it Plugged in?

One of the first questions anyone troubleshooting anything with a plug or cable should ask is, "Is it plugged in?" We are going to assume that your computer is operating correctly at this point. That is not always a good assumption, but troubleshooting all computer problems is beyond the scope of this book. Therefore, the question applies to the network cable, and not the computer's power cord.

One of the simplest ways to make sure your computer has a good connection is to simply unplug the cable at both ends, and plug the connector back in again, making sure the connection feels solid. It is not necessary to turn the computer off when plugging or unplugging network cables. In fact, there is some advantage to leaving the computer running when troubleshooting a network connection. You can take advantage of the network card's built-in troubleshooting system of lights.

All NICs have small LEDs that indicate when a network link to another network device is achieved. The manufacturer probably has a technical name for these small lights, but referring to them as *link lights* is easiest. Looking in the back of your computer, where your network cable plugs into the card, you should see the link lights illuminate when the network cable is plugged into another network device, and both devices, including another computer, a hub, or router, is turned on.

Having link lights turned on (illuminated) does not mean that the network cable is functioning properly. Having them turned off, however, is the best indication that the network cable is not making a good connection. This could be due to several possible problems:

• The network cable is bad. The connector may be damaged or the cable may be cut or broken internally.

• The NIC card may have failed.

• The device to which you are attaching your computer may have failed.

This is not a long list but it will require some patience to work through each possibility. The first possible problem is checked easiest by replacing the network cable. If your computer is in a different room from the device to which you are connecting, it may be easiest to move your computer into the same room temporarily rather than string a new network cable. Use a network cable you know to be working correctly and connect it to the device. If this solves your network problem, you will need to replace your network cable.

 Note: When a network cable fails to operate, you must keep in mind the maximum distance a network cable may be in length. Refer to Chapter 4 for that information.

Additional Hardware Issues

If you try to connect a network cable you know to be working properly and you still have no link lights, open the computer and check that your NIC card is properly seated in the expansion slot. You *must* turn off your computer to perform this check.

After reseating the network card, turn the computer back on. If an incorrectly seated network card was the problem, the link lights should come on.

Remember that your computer may not be the problem. If you are connecting to a network hub, try changing the port in the hub to which the computer is connected. You can also try connecting to a network card of another computer. If all of these endeavors fail to illuminate the link lights, you should consider that the network card has failed and needs to be replaced.

One final note about link lights—100baseT cards usually have twice the number of link lights as comparable 10baseT cards, indicating the higher speed of the card. When connecting a 100baseT NIC card to a 10baseT device, you may see only half the link lights illuminate, indicating that the NIC is operating at 10baseT speeds—not that there might be a problem.

Tools for Hardware Troubleshooting

You can purchase an inexpensive test unit for testing a network cable. The Network Tone Probe and Tone Generator (Figure 9.1) allows you to check the health of your network cable by plugging the cable into the tone generator and testing the other end of the cable to detect a tone. When tone is not present, a continuous signal does not exist and the cable or cable ends are faulty.

There are fancier probes that allow you to plug your computer or hub directly into the probe to test the communications health of your device. A standard tone generator and tone probe cost around $70. When adding more features to your test device, the cost begins to double and triple.

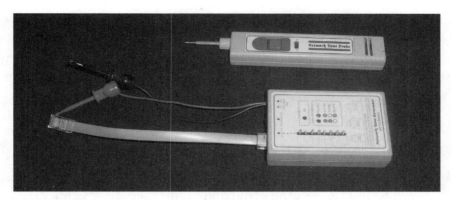

Figure 9.1 *Network Tone Generator and Tone Probe.*

Configuration Troubles

After determining that your hardware is physically connected, the next step is to check your computer's network configuration. Notice that we said that your hardware is connected. This still does not mean that your network card is functioning correctly, just correctly enough to display link lights. This will be mentioned again in the When All Else Fails section.

Your network-software configuration enables your computer to maintain an IP address and communicate over the network. Every computer on the network must have an IP address. If your computer is behind a firewall, it will probably have a local IP address, normally starting with 127. Your computer might also have an Internet IP address. The IP address of your computer is either set during configuration, or established by contacting a DHCP server and requesting one. Many broadband and dial-up Internet accounts require you to request an IP address via DHCP. If your computer is having difficulty contacting your ISP, or your ISP is having difficulty communicating with your computer, the ISP's DHCP server may not have correctly issued an IP address.

You should first check to see what your computer thinks its IP address is. This value may be different from what you have configured in your network settings. Check your computer's IP address using one of the methods described in the following sections.

IPConfig

If your computer is running Windows 2000 or XP, you can use the IPConfig utility to view your computer's IP address information. Follow these steps to start IPConfig:

1. From the Start menu, choose Programs.

2. Select the Command Prompt utility and start it.

3. From the command prompt, type ipconfig and hit Enter.

Your computer's IP address, subnet mask, and the IP address of the default gateway will be displayed in the command prompt windows as follows:

```
Windows 2000 IP Configuration



Ethernet adapter Local Area Connection:



   Connection-specific DNS Suffix  . :
   IP Address. . . . . . . . . . . : 65.13.78.192
   Subnet Mask . . . . . . . . . . : 255.255.255.0
   Default Gateway . . . . . . . . : 65.13.78.1
the IPConfig program can display additional information.
   Include /all parameter when running IPConfig.


Ipconfig /all
```

Additional information displayed is shown in Table 9.1.

Table 9.1 Full IP Configuration Information

Information Type	Description
Host Name	The textual host name of your computer
Primary DNS Suffix	The FQDN of this computer if it has one, otherwise it is blank
Node Type	Unknown or Hybrid
IP Routing Enabled	Yes if IP routing enabled, otherwise No
WINS Proxy Enabled	Yes if WINS Proxy is enabled, otherwise No
DNS Suffix Search List	The FQDN of this computer if it has one, otherwise it is blank
Connection-specific DNS Suffix	Setting for resolution of unqualified domain names(see note)
Description	Description of Ethernet card
Physical Address	MAC address of Ethernet card
DHCP Enabled	Yes if the computer obtains an IP address via DHCP, otherwise No
IP Address	The IP address assigned to this computer
Subnet Mask	The subnet mask assigned to this computer
Default Gateway	The IP address of the default gateway
DNS Servers	List of DNS servers configured for this computer

Note: An unqualified domain name is one that does not contain the three elements of a domain name: the host, the domain, and the domain suffix. Many computer applications, such as e-mail programs, recognize unqualified domain names and attempt to turn them into FQDNs by appending the domain and domain suffix.

WinIPCFG

Computers running Windows 95, 98, or Me should use the WinIPCFG utility. There are a few extra steps when using WinIPCfg compared to using IPConfig:

1. From the Start menu, choose Run.

2. In the Run dialog, type winipcfg and click OK.

3. In the IP Configuration window that appears, select your ethernet card from the dropdown list found in the Ethernet Adapter information block.

You can then view the ethernet card's MAC address, the IP address, subnet mask, and default gateway IP address.

An alternative way to find your computer's IP address is to view the computer's routing table using the Netstat utility.

Netstat

The Netstat utility program can display information about the state of your computer's network connection. To run the Netstat utility, follow these steps:

1. From the Start menu, choose Programs.
2. Select the Command Prompt utility and start it.
3. From the command prompt, type Netstat -r and hit Enter.

The Netstat program will display five columns of information as shown in Table 9.2.

Table 9.2 Output of Netstat program

Network Address	Netmask	Gateway	Interface	Metric
0.0.0.0	0.0.0.0	65.13.78.1	65.13.78.192	1
65.13.78.0	255.255.255.0	65.13.78.192	65.13.78.192	1
65.13.78.192	255.255.255.255	127.0.0.1	127.0.0.1	1
65.255.255.255	255.255.255.255	65.13.78.192	65.13.78.192	1
127.0.0.0	255.0.0.0	127.0.0.1	127.0.0.1	1
224.0.0.0	224.0.0.0	65.13.78.192	65.13.78.192	1
255.255.255.255	255.255.255.255	65.13.78.192	65.13.78.192	1

The information displayed by Netstat will be specific to your computer's network configuration. The —r tells Netstat to display your computer's routing table. Your computer's IP address is found in this routing table. There are several different IP addresses and netmasks in the routing table and it can be confusing. You can find your computer's IP address in the first row in the column labeled Interface. For example, in Table 9.2, the computer's IP address is 65.13.78.192.

Testing the Connection

Once you have determined that your computer is physically connected to the network and properly configured, you can test the network connection using a very useful utility known as Ping.

The Ping program sends out a small packet, called a datagram, out over the Internet. As the datagram is sent, the sending machine notes the exact time. The datagram is routed to a destination machine which constructs an echo reply and sends it back. The computer that is sending out ping packets notes the time of the returned datagram and prints Ping output.

To run Ping follow these steps:

1. From the Start menu, choose Programs.

2. Select the Command Prompt utility and start it.

3. From the command prompt, type ping and the IP address or domain name of the target, then hit Enter.

Typing ping yahoo.com at the command prompt results in the following:

```
Pinging yahoo.com [216.115.109.7] with 32 bytes of data:



Reply from 216.115.109.7: bytes=32 time=30ms TTL=241

Reply from 216.115.109.7: bytes=32 time=30ms TTL=241

Reply from 216.115.109.7: bytes=32 time=31ms TTL=241

Reply from 216.115.109.7: bytes=32 time=30ms TTL=241



Ping statistics for 216.115.109.7:
```

(continued)

```
    Packets: Sent = 4, Received = 4, Lost = 0 (0% loss),

Approximate round trip times in milli-seconds:

Minimum = 30ms, Maximum =  31ms, Average =  30ms
```

You can see from the Ping results that the round trip took about 30 milliseconds from our computer to yahoo.com and back. It also makes three ping attempts.

It is possible to tell the Ping program to continue pinging until told to stop. Include the **–t** argument on the command line as follows:

```
ping -t
```

To stop the Ping program, hit the Ctrl-c key combination on your keyboard. For a full list of all the Ping command line arguments type

```
ping /?
```

The Story of Ping

Ping was written by Mike Muus in December of 1983 as an add-on utility for the UNIX operating system. It was a little thousand-line program written to help troubleshoot a network problem. This little program has become one of the most used network utilities ever, and in Mike's own words, "If I'd known then that it would be my most famous accomplishment in life, I might have worked on it another day or two and added some more options."

Sadly, Michael John Muuss was killed in an automobile accident on US Route 95 in Maryland, November 20, 2000.

You can supply either a domain name or an IP address to the Ping program. When supplying a domain name, a DNS lookup is performed. You can see the IP address of the target computer displayed by the Ping program.

If you can ping another computer over the network, you are successfully connected. If your ping returns a message that says Request Timed Out, it does not necessarily mean that you are not connected to the network, it just means your computer cannot see the remote computer. You should then try pinging a machine on your local network, and not on the Internet. If you cannot ping a local machine, either your computer or the one you are trying to ping is not connected to the network.

Tracing the Connection Path

The Traceroute utility allows you to trace the path your network packets take along the route to their destination. This is useful when you are successfully connected to a network, or even the Internet, and find that you cannot contact a particular computer on the network. It is also useful when you think that the connection to the remote computer appears to be slow You can see every *hop* your packet takes to its destination.

To run the Traceroute utility follow these steps:

1. From the Start menu, choose Programs.

2. Select the Command Prompt utility and start it.

3. From the command prompt, type tracert and the destination IP address or domain name, then hit Enter.

The Traceroute program will begin displaying each hop the network packet is taking along its route to the specified destination. The following is a sample output from the Traceroute program:

```
Tracing route to yahoo.com [216.115.109.6]

over a maximum of 30 hops:



     1     50 ms     30 ms     20 ms   65.13.78.195
```

(continued)

2	20 ms	20 ms	20 ms	4.24.148.137
3	20 ms	20 ms	20 ms	4.24.207.1
4	20 ms	20 ms	20 ms	4.25.111.6
5	20 ms	20 ms	20 ms	209.0.227.57
6	40 ms	30 ms	20 ms	209.247.10.193
7	30 ms	30 ms	30 ms	209.247.9.114
8	80 ms	30 ms	30 ms	64.159.2.138
9	431 ms	340 ms	30 ms	64.152.81.62
10	30 ms	100 ms	30 ms	216.115.101.42
11	30 ms	30 ms	40 ms	216.115.100.229
12	80 ms	30 ms	40 ms	216.115.109.6

Trace complete.

If your connection is interrupted anywhere along the path, or if your trace requires more than thirty hops, you will not see your packets reach their destination. When the trace stops before reaching thirty hops with a result that appears like the following:

```
8 *    *   * Request timed out
```

You know that the packets are not reaching their destination and that the entry on the line just before this one contains the address of the last hop along the destination. This allows you to see where the connection is failing. Once you know where the connection is failing you will know whether the problem exists on your network, or out on the Internet. As durable and resilient as the Internet is, it is still prone to failure. There have been occasions where construction workers have accidentally severed major Internet trunk lines affecting millions of Internet subscribers. If the problem is on your network, you can take the appropriate action such as replacing a bad cable or a bad network card, or correcting the software configuration.

Assorted Network Problems

Some network problems are simple to solve. The following are some of the problems you may run into and their solutions.

IP Conflict

After installing your computer on the network, you may get an IP Conflict error message. This means that another computer on the network has already been assigned the IP address you have assigned to your computer. Either change the IP address in your computer or determine which other computer on the network is conflicting and change its IP address. All IP addresses on a network must be unique.

No Computers Appear in Network Neighborhood

You have successfully connected your computer on the network but no other computers appear in your Windows Network Neighborhood.

You must install the NetBEUI protocol to view computers or share files and printers with other computers through Network Neighborhood. To install NetBEUI follow these steps:

1. Start the Control Panel applet.

2. Start the Network applet.

3. Modify the properties of your LAN.

4. Click the Install button in the Local Area Connection Properties dialog. This launches the Select Network Component Type dialog.

5. Click the Protocol selection and click the Add button. This launches the Select Network Protocol dialog.

6. Select NetBEUI Protocol. Click the OK button. This will begin the installation of the NetBEUI protocol. You may be required to place your Windows CD in the CD-ROM drive during this installation. You will be required to reboot after installation.

The Wireless Connection is Slow or Intermittent

There are two primary causes for slow and intermittent wireless network connections. The first, and most common problem, is signal strength. Most wireless networks require a fairly unobstructed path between the wireless transceiver and the wireless NIC. Sometimes it is difficult to determine what will and will not obstruct the signal. For example, most interior walls will not obstruct the signal. This is true unless the interior wall happens to be brick or cinderblock. This type of solid interior wall can cause the signal of your wireless network to be degraded.

To solve this problem you may have to move the location of your wireless transceiver or computer with the wireless NIC installed. Test the connection using Ping (explained earlier in this chapter). Using ping –t allows your ping to continue endlessly until manually stopped. For this procedure it helps to have a friend monitor the ping while you move the wireless transceiver. When the ping appears steady, and connection times are reduced, you have maximized your wireless connection.

Another reason why you may experience temporary wireless-network failure is radio-frequency interference. Devices in your home may broadcast radio signals at or near the same frequency as your wireless network. Some of the devices to be aware of are

- Microwave ovens
- Wireless telephones
- Amateur radio broadcasting equipment
- Electric motors, especially heavy duty motors such as pool and spa pumps

Remember, if you live in an apartment, the interference may be coming from equipment in your neighbor's apartment. While most wireless networks have a frequency-hopping ability to overcome interference, you have to isolate your network from this equipment if the problems persist.

When All Else Fails

When you are just about to pull your hair out, and you are certain that your computer is configured correctly, the network cable just came out of the package, the network card is seated correctly, but you still do not have a connection, one of two things is probably wrong. Either you do not have the software drivers for the network card installed correctly or the network card has failed and must be replaced.

To see if the driver software is installed and operating correctly, follow these steps:

1. From the Start menu, choose Settings.
2. Select Control Panel. This will launch the Control Panel applet.
3. In the Control Panel, double click the System icon. This will launch the System Properties dialog.
4. In the System Properties Dialog, select the Hardware tab.
5. Click the Device Manager button. This launches the Device Manager dialog as shown in Figure 9.2.
6. Expand the section titled Network adapters by clicking the small + sign.
7. If you see a network card listed, a driver was installed. To see if the driver is operating correctly, continue to step 8.
8. Right-click on the name of the network card and select Properties from the popup menu. This launches the Properties window for the NIC as shown in Figure 9.3.

If the device is operating correctly, you will see a message similar to the one shown in Figure 9.3. If the device is not operating correctly, you will see an error message.

If you are having difficulties, you can click the Troubleshooter button and Windows will help you troubleshoot the problem.

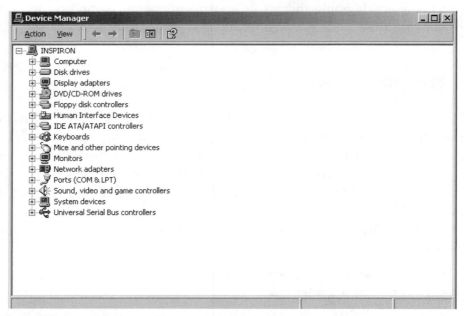

Figure 9.2 *View device driver status in the Device Manager dialog.*

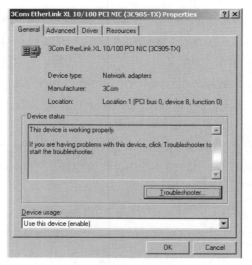

Figure 9.3 *The NIC Properties dialog will tell you if the device driver is functioning properly.*

Rather than open the NIC Properties window, you can also choose to uninstall the device driver. Once the device driver is uninstalled you should reboot your computer. The plug-and-play feature of Windows should recognize your network card and attempt to reinstall the device driver. If you have the disk that came with the network card, it is always best to use the driver that comes with the card.

When all else fails, try replacing the NIC in your computer. Like all other electronics, they can fail. Remember to remove the power cord from the back of your computer before installing or uninstalling boards into the expansion slot. This is not important just for your safety, but also because the power supply keeps sending a certain amount of electricity to the expansion boards, even when the computer is turned off. Plugging or unplugging a board with the power cord in place can damage your computer and/or the expansion card.

Summary

Troubleshooting networks is not difficult; it just requires patience and a structured approach. Unlike troubleshooting software problems, network problems are a little bit more difficult to find unless you know where to look. The information provided in this chapter is enough to solve just about any home-networking problem.

Home of the Future 10

The home of the future is not that far in the future. In fact, it is here now—you just have to know where to find the equipment to make your home the sci-fi home of your dreams. Essentially, when you think about the electronic devices available for your home and how they integrate with your home network you should consider the following:

- Video and home entertainment systems
- Security, fire, and protection systems
- Telephone and voice communications
- Home automation of such things as lighting, heating, and cooling
- Home office and home education systems
- Transportation such as your car, truck, or motorcycle

Everything from television sets and set top boxes to your refrigerator can now be connected to your home network. This chapter introduces some of the new, networked home appliances, digital phone systems, security systems, home automation systems, and online entertainment systems. Kids and game enthusiasts will be excited to learn about which game systems allow them to play with others across the Internet or over their home network.

Universal Plug and Play

To create the interconnected world of the future, a standard was required. Equipment vendors of all types—home security companies, computer manufacturers, consumer electronics companies, and companies that make products such as printers, digital cameras and home appliances—formed an organization to create such a standard. The standard is known as Universal Plug and Play (UPNP) (*www.upnp.org*).

What is UPNP? UPNP is software that has the ability to automatically recognize devices (such as computers, scanners, appliances, etc) when they are connected to a "residential gateway" so that these devices can communicate with each other.

Cisco and 3Com have postponed their plans to develop the residential gateways for now. They believe that consumers are more worried about sharing printers and scanners than appliances. The residential gateways will be crucial components for the connectivity of the different appliances and equipment around the house.

New wireless products are now under development using a new chipset that incorporates both Wi-Fi and Bluetooth technologies.

Home Automation

Cisco, a large network equipment manufacturer has worked with familiar home-appliance companies such as Whirlpool to develop next-generation products and services. Many of the new appliances being developed for the home will have the ability to communicate with each other over a home network and communicate over the Internet to perform tasks such as automatic software and firmware upgrades, service requests and diagnostics, or less "self-centered" tasks such as shopping for food (Figure 10.1) or setting your air-conditioning system based on developing weather patterns.

The Korean company, LG Electronics Inc. (*http://www.lge.com*) is making news with its new line of Internet-ready home appliances. The following sections describe some of the products.

Digital Multimedia Side-By-Side Fridge Freezer with LCD Display

What more can you expect from your refrigerator other than to store your food, keep it fresh, and possibly supply some chilled water and ice? Well the GRD-267DTV fridge, from LG Electronics, can do that and more. This high-tech refrigerator is not only Internet-ready but is PDA and cell-phone compatible. You can call this unit from the store and ask it to tell you what you need.

This high-tech refrigerator maintains an automated inventory that can tell you what you have with out opening the door. No more hunting for expiration dates or moldy cream cheese—it also keeps track of how long food has been stored. Believe it or not this unit will even warn you when you are running low in a product—for example, when you are almost out of milk.

Figure 10.1 *Next-generation refrigerators will do your shopping.*

Also, it is not just for keeping things cold! It comes with a 15-inch LCD display, stereo, and digital camera. You can watch your favorite films on this cable and Internet-ready, radio-ready entertainment system and can even play MP3s. These are only some of the fun features. We have not even mentioned the state-of-the-art technology to keep your food fresh.

Air Conditioning System

You can control the temperature of your house over the Internet or just call on the phone and add a few degrees for those cold winter nights. You have complete remote control of your home's climate-control system by network or cell phone. You can turn the unit on and off or make adjustments remotely. The LG Electronics Air Conditioner can also contact you when the self-diagnostics software senses a problem. Your home network can expand to allow devices like your air conditioner to be a part of your home network, and your cell phone to act as a network terminal.

Gadgets

The imagination is the only limit to the types of household appliances that either now connect to your home network or will soon. LG Electronics is already working on an Internet-ready microwave and washing machine. Games and home-entertainment systems are already attachable to your home network. It does not take much imagination to see what is possible. Take the following scenario, for example.

You are driving home from work and you call the house to get the dinner you placed in the oven cooking. The thermostat also adjusts a couple of degrees and the refrigerator cuts in to remind you to pick up some butter. You drive into your driveway and the garage-door remote sends your private key to the garage door opener which signals the home-security unit to disengage and alerts the network to your arrival.

The home security system knows you are in the garage and senses the door entry into the house. A soft voice asks you if you would like to hear your messages or read them in e-mail. A biosensor notices that your heart rate is elevated and adjusts ambient music and lighting to add a calming affect. You sit down to scan your e-mail and notice that your dog has logged in and sent you an instant message alerting you to the fact that he has not been fed, and that he successfully guarded the house against intruders.

The previous example is largely fiction, but Xanboo Inc. (*http://www.xanboo.com*), a New York-based company, claims to have "created the first smart home management system with real-time video notification and device control that enables users to control and monitor their home or businesses from anywhere in the world, via the Internet." The Xanboo products are used to monitor the systems in your home. It is not a security system but it may help determine when something in your house is amiss. Some of the products that Xanboo is currently selling are

- **Xanboo System Controller** – This is the main unit which connects to a PC and receives and processes the signals for all of the other Xanboo products.

- **Xanboo Color Video Camera** – This video camera has a built-in motion sensor and microphone. It can take video or still pictures every ten seconds.

- **Xanboo Acoustic Sensor** – The sensor detects sound between 70 and 100 decibels.

- **Xanboo Door/Window Sensor** – This sensor monitors when doors or windows are opened.

- **Xanboo Power On/Off Sensor** – This sensor detects when there is a power failure in your appliances or machines.

- **Xanboo Temperature Sensor** – This sensor monitors the temperature of the surrounding area where the sensor is situated.

- **Xanboo Water Sensor** – This sensor detects if the water level has risen higher than 1/8 of an inch—it is used to detect leaky refrigerators, washing machines, dishwashers, broken pipes, and so on.

All of the Xanboo products are controlled by the System Controller, which is connected to a PC via a USB cable. The Xanboo software processes all of the information from the System Controller. Information from the sensors is available over the Internet to the owner through the Xanboo Web site. Xanboo requires a small fee to access your sensors remotely through their site. Xanboo is preparing a new line of control products that will be available soon. These products are less passive and will allow remote users to control systems in their home over a network. Some of the new products will be: Power On/Off control switch, Temperature Control, Water Control, Garage Door Control, and Pool Shark (monitors pools PH, temperature, and excessive movement).

Video

The ability to broadcast high-quality home video over your broadband network connection is becoming a reality. DSL providers will soon be competing with cable companies to provide you with quality digital programming. You will soon hear of standards such as MPEG-4 and H.26L which offer video compression as high as 400 percent greater than current MPEG-2 standards in current use according to a March 26, 2002 article on CNN.com.

Some cars already have DVD players installed. It is only a matter of time until movies can be downloaded via satellite straight to the car.

Home Game Consoles

Just as with other familiar home appliances, video games will also be an integral part of your home network. Home game consoles like Sony's Playstation 2 and Microsoft's Xbox are introducing network capabilities to the console market. You can play against other people on your own network or over the Internet.

Neither of these two major gaming consoles is Internet ready, but both can be used over your home network.

Sony's PS2 Broadband, (not available in the United States at the time of publication) allows Playstation 2 users to download movies, games, and music from the Internet. Using the Playstation 2 USB ports you can connect to a USB network adapter or modem. You will have to refer to the console's technical documentation to determine which network adapters are compatible.

The Xbox Gateway is a third-party Internet service that enables Xbox users to interconnect using special software that acts as an ethernet gateway between game consoles. This allows games with System Link functionality to be played between users over the Internet. The Xbox has an ethernet port built-in, ready to use and connect to other computers or Xboxes.

Nintendo's Gamecube will soon enter the market for broadband games. You will be able to buy an adapter for your Gamecube, choosing between an ethernet adapter and a 56K modem adapter.

As toys become part of the network, you might be able to control them from your computer. Imagine the following:

You: "Kids it's 10 PM, time to turn the game off and go to bed"

Kids: "But we are in the last level, it will only take three more hours to finish the game."

You: "Ok, save the game because I am shutting it down in five minutes."

Five minutes later you reach into your Control Panel, you see the game connection, and CLICK!—disconnected.

Kids: "DAD!!!"

You: "Good night."

Wireless Roaming

Imagine you have installed an 802.11 wireless network in your house that allows you to grab your laptop and walk around the house unhindered by network cables, perhaps even into your own backyard—but then what? There is a new system being built that will allow your 802.11 devices to roam while directly connected to the cellular telephone network. This connection is different from the low-speed wireless connection you can achieve with wireless modems. This is a direct wireless network connection exactly like the one you have in home networks.

Currently available only in Europe for the GSM-based phone system, this technology will soon migrate to the United States-based CDMA digital cellular system.

The Car

Your car is an extension of your home, and for those who commute in large cities, it probably feels like home. The automobile has remained relatively unchanged over the last 70 years. You have an engine, some lights, and a radio. Yes, it is true that cars are now computer controlled, and even the braking systems on cars are microprocessor controlled. It is only now, however, that we seeing a *real* revolution in auto technology.

Global Positioning Systems (GPS) guide drivers with maps, even vocally telling a driver when to make a turn to reach a destination. GPS systems are no longer one-way location finders. Systems like OnStar send help and human remote assistance by using the information from a built-in GPS. It will not be long before cars are self-guided by systems similar to GPS.

The car's audio system has changed over the years. It has migrated from AM to FM, from tape to CD. Now, your system can play traditional CDs or music CDs recorded on your home computer or play MP3 music files downloaded from the Internet. Some of the newest models can even play DVDs, displaying the image on small liquid-crystal displays.

Computers in the Car

PCs for the car are now available. When you have that nagging question and wish you were in front of your computer at home so you could log into the Internet, you will have the computer right there in the car. Fitting into the slot where you would find your car radio, these small PCs integrate much of the technology mentioned earlier. The PC will integrate with a GPS to give you driving directions, play CDs and MP3 files, and provide functions like retrieving your e-mail and other features you would expect from a regular computer.

There are ways the computer in your car can be connected to your network at home, even allowing access to the files on your home computer. You can create Virtual Private Networks (VPN) that will give you safe and secure access to your home network just as though you were right in the house (or garage).

Out There

The people who brought you Virtual Reality (VR) have not been sucked into a computer somewhere, living out their lives in a bit stream as some movies suggest. Instead they are working on ways to bring education and collaboration remotely to places like your office or bedroom. The technology, in its current state, requires a level of Internet access only available in universities and research laboratories like the one at NTII (*http://www.advanced.org*).

Figure 10.2 shows the workplace of the future—perhaps it is not too different from what you may have in your home office. The researcher in the photo is holding a vase that will be included as an object in the virtual world shown in Figure 10.3. Notice that the bookcases and filing cabinets shown in the virtual world do not exist in the physical world.

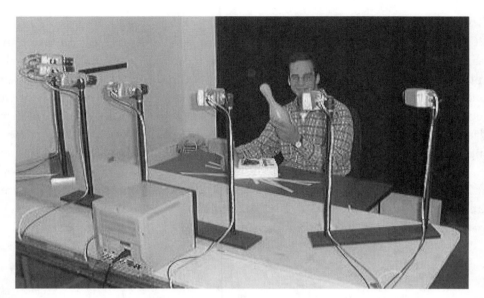

Figure 10.2 *Immersion Workplace in real life.*

Figure 10.3 *Immersion Workplace as seen in a virtual world.*

Pen Tablets: Notebooks of the Future?

Companies such as Fujitsu are developing pen tablets with the same capabilities that notebooks had only a year ago. Pen tablets are starting to get very popular. They are thin, light, compact, and they are becoming more powerful with each new generation. The latest Fujitsu Stylistic 3500R Pen tablets have a 500 MHz Intel Celeron processor, 256 MB of SDRAM and a 15 GB hard drive. The tablet is equipped with a 10.4-inch Reflective SVGA LCD display, a built-in modem, and a 10/100 ethernet adapter. Also included are all the ports to connect a mouse, keyboard, and USB devices. The only big difference between a tablet and a notebook computer so far is the price (see Table 10.1). As soon as tablets come down in price they may very likely replace notebook computers. The pen tablet is the type of computer you currently see used in the 24th century sci-fi TV show, Star Trek.

Table 10.1 Comparison Between Fujitsu Notebooks and Pen Tablets

Component	Pen Tablets		Notebooks	
	Stylistic 3500R	Stylistec LT P-600F	E Series	P-1000
Processor	500MHz Inte1 Celeron	600 MHz Intel Pentium III	700 MHz Crusoe TM5500	1.2 GHz-M Mobile Intel Pentium III
Video	10.4" reflective SVGA TFT	8.4" transflective SVGA TFT	8.9" wide-format XGA TFT with touch screen	14.1" XGA TFT
Memory	256 MB SDRAM	256 MB SDRAM	128 MB memory	256 MB memory
Hard drive	15 GB shock mounted	15 GB	20 GB	30 GB
Modem	56K modem	56K modem	56K modem	
Network Card	10/100 Mbps ethernet	10/100 Mbps ethernet	10/100 Mbps ethernet	10/100 Mbps ethernet

Table 10.1 Comparison Between Fujitsu Notebooks and Pen Tablets *(continued)*

Component	Pen Tablets		Notebooks	
Dimensions	11.0"(W) 8.5"(D) 1.1"(H) 3.2 lbs.	9.6" (W) 6.3" (D) 1.1" (H) 2.65 lbs.	9.1"(W) 6.5"(D) 1.36"(H) 2.5 lbs.	12.13"(W) 10.39"(D) 1.52"(H) 5.8 lbs.
Other features	Sound Blaster ATI Rage Mobility USB ports Stereo headphone jack Microphone jack Floppy drive port Keyboard port Serial port Mouse port	Sound Blaster ATI Rage Mobility USB ports CardBus PC Card slot Compact Flash slot Microphone jack Headphones jack Wireless IR keyboard port Keyboard port Mouse port	SigmaTel STAC 9723 16-bit stereo audio Two stereo speakers ATI Rage Mobility USB ports Only Type II or Type II card slot 32-bit PC CardBus card slot External USB floppy drive External PCM-CIA CD-ROM Headphone jack Microphone jack	SigmaTel STAC 9723 16-bit stereo audio Dolby Headphone utility ATI Mobility RAdeon D USB ports Support for external monitor and internal display External USB floppy drive DVD/CD-RW combo Wireless mouse Full-size keyboard Two Type II or Type II card slots 32-bit PC CardBus card slot Embedded Smart Card Reader
Price	$3,659	$3,659	$1,499	$2,399

A related technology that is improving is handwriting-recognition software. The Microsoft Office XP product offers a handwriting recognition add-in product.

Another holy grail for human interface with the computer is voice recognition. Faster hardware has enabled voice recognition to finally become ready for prime time. It is strange enough to see people walking down the street apparently talking to themselves as they speak into hands-free cell phones. Think how strange it will be when people start talking to their notepad computers!

Summary

This chapter has discussed some of the latest technologies and some that are still on the near horizon. They may not seem a part of your current home network plans but it is smart when installing a new network to consider how you might take advantage of new technologies in the next three to five years. This is particularly true if you are deciding whether to install copper or fiber optic cable in the wall. It is not as big an issue if you are choosing a wireless network, as that is more easily changed and adapted. Chances are good that all of the devices discussed in this chapter and many that have not even been dreamed of yet will be able to interact on a standard TCP/IP home network.

Have fun with your network. Take good care of it and it will take good care of you.

Appendix

IP Address Allocations

Address Block	Purpose
000/8	IANA – Reserved
001/8	IANA – Reserved
002/8	IANA – Reserved
003/8	General Electric Company
004/8	Bolt Beranek and Newman Inc.
005/8	IANA – Reserved
006/8	Army Information Systems Center
007/8	IANA – Reserved
008/8	Bolt Beranek and Newman Inc.
009/8	IBM
010/8	IANA – Private Use
011/8	DoD Intel Information Systems
012/8	AT&T Bell Laboratories
013/8	Xerox Corporation
014/8	IANA – Public Data Network
015/8	Hewlett-Packard Company
016/8	Digital Equipment Corporation
017/8	Apple Computer Inc.
018/8	MIT
019/8	Ford Motor Company
020/8	Computer Sciences Corporation
021/8	DDN-RVN
022/8	Defense Information Systems Agency
023/8	IANA – Reserved

IP Address Allocations *(continued)*

Address Block	Purpose
024/8	ARIN – Cable Block
025/8	Royal Signals and Radar Establishment
026/8	Defense Information Systems Agency
027/8	IANA – Reserved
028/8	DSI–North
029/8	Defense Information Systems Agency
030/8	Defense Information Systems Agency
031/8	IANA – Reserved
032/8	Norsk Informasjonsteknologi
033/8	DLA Systems Automation Center
034/8	Halliburton Company
035/8	MERIT Computer Network
036/8	IANA – Reserved (Formerly Stanford University – Apr 93)
037/8	IANA – Reserved
038/8	Performance Systems International
039/8	IANA – Reserved
040/8	Eli Lily and Company
041/8	IANA – Reserved
042/8	IANA – Reserved
043/8	Japan Inet
044/8	Amateur Radio Digital Communications
045/8	Interop Show Network
046/8	Bolt Beranek and Newman Inc.
047/8	Bell–Northern Research
048/8	Prudential Securities Inc.
049/8	Joint Technical Command Returned to IANA
050/8	Joint Technical Command Returned to IANA
051/8	Deparment of Social Security of UK
052/8	E.I. duPont de Nemours and Co., Inc.
053/8	Cap Debis CCS

IP Address Allocations *(continued)*

Address Block	Purpose
054/8	Merck and Co., Inc.
055/8	Boeing Computer Services
056/8	U.S. Postal Service
057/8	SITA
058/8	IANA – Reserved
059/8	IANA – Reserved
060/8	IANA – Reserved
061/8	APNIC – Pacific Rim
062/8	RIPE NCC – Europe
063/8	ARIN
064/8	ARIN
065/8	ARIN
066/8	ARIN
067/8	ARIN
068/8	ARIN
069–079/8	
080/8	RIPE NCC
081/8	RIPE NCC
082–095/8	
096–126/8	
127/8	IANA – Reserved
128–191/8	
192/8	Various Registries – MultiRegional
193/8	RIPE NCC – Europe
194/8	RIPE NCC – Europe
195/8	RIPE NCC – Europe
196/8	Various Registries
197/8	IANA – Reserved
198/8	Various Registries
199/8	ARIN – North America
200/8	ARIN – Central and South America
201/8	Reserved – Central and South America
202/8	APNIC – Pacific Rim

IP Address Allocations *(continued)*

Address Block	Purpose	
203/8	APNIC – Pacific Rim	
204/8	ARIN – North America	
205/8	ARIN – North America	
206/8	ARIN – North America	
207/8	ARIN – North America	
208/8	ARIN – North America	
209/8	ARIN – North America	
210/8	APNIC – Pacific Rim	
211/8	APNIC – Pacific Rim	
212/8	RIPE NCC – Europe	Oct 97
213/8	RIPE NCC – Europe	Mar 99
214/8	US-DOD	
215/8	US-DOD	Mar 98
216/8	ARIN – North America	Apr 98
217/8	RIPE NCC – Europe	Jun 00
218/8	APNIC – Pacific Rim	
219-223/	8 IANA – Reserved	
224-239/8		
240-255/8		

Where To Go For More Information

Consult the following Web sites for more information regarding networks:

3 Com (*http://www.3com.com*)

About.com (*http://www.about.com*)

ActionLink (*http://www.actiontec.com*)

Airport Technology (*http://www.apple.com/airport/*)

Broadband Reports (*http://www.dslreports.com*)

Charles Spurgeon's Ethernet Site
     (*http://www.ethermanage.com/ethernet/ethernet.html*)

Delmar Learning (*http://www.delmar.com*)

DIY home networking guides (*http://www.homenethelp.com/*)

Everything DSL (*http://www.everythingdsl.com/*)

EZ-Link Instant Network (*http://www.ezlinkusb.com*)

Furman Sound Web site (*http://www.furmansound.com/BalPwr.html*)

HardwareCentral (*http://www.hardwarecentral.com*)

Home Networking Help (*http://www.home-networking-help.com/*)

HomePNA (*http://www.homepna.com*)

HomeRF (*http://www.homerf.org*)

How StuffWorks (*http://www.howstuffworks.com/*)

Iomega (*http://www.iomega.com*)

LG Electronics Inc. (*http://www.lge.com*)

Linksys (*http://www.linksys.com*)

Lockdown Trojan protection (*http://www.lockdowncorp.com/*)

McAfee (*http://www.mcafee.com/*)

MSN Messenger visit (*http://messenger.msn.com/*)

Norton Anti-Virus (*http://www.symantec.com/*)

NTII (*http://www.advanced.org*)

Panda Software (*http://www.pandasoftware.com*)

Proxim (*http://www.proxim.com*)

ShareWave (*http://www.sharewave.com*)

SimpleDevices (*http://www.simpledevices.com*)

The HomeHELP Network (*http://www.homehelpnet.com/*)

Unibrain (*http://www.unibrain.com*)

Universal Plug and Play (*http://www.upnp.org*)

USB (*http://www.usb.org*)

Webopedia (*http://www.webopedia.com*)

What is? (*http://whatis.com*)

WildPacket Airo Peed (*http://www.wildpackets.com/products/airopeek*)

Windows XP (*http://www.microsoft.com/windowsxp/default.asp*)

Xanboo Inc. (*http://www.xanboo.com*)

100baseT
A standard for 100 Mb network packet communications.

10baseT
A standard for 10 Mb network packet communications.

2.4 GHz
Speed of some wireless networks and portable phones. This speed is considered to be in the microwave radio frequency.

56 k
The data throughput speed of a standard narrow-band modem. A standard, narrow band modem is one connected to a phone line and is different than a broadband DSL or cable modem.

802.11, 802.11a, or 802.11b *see Wi-Fi*

A

ad-hoc mode
An 802.11 networking framework in which devices or stations communicate directly with each other, without the use of an Access Point (AP). Ad-hoc mode is also referred to as peer-to-peer mode or an Independent Basic Service Set (IBSS). Ad-hoc mode is useful for establishing a network in which wireless infrastructure does not exist or in which services are not required.

Address Resolution Protocol (ARP)
A TCP/IP protocol used to convert an IP address into a physical address (called a DLC address), such as an ethernet address. A host wishing to obtain a physical address broadcasts an ARP request onto the TCP/IP network. The host on the network that has the IP address in the request then replies with its physical hardware address.

Access Point (AP)
A hardware device or a computer's software that acts as a communication hub for users of a wireless device to connect to a wired Local Area Network (LAN). APs are important for providing heightened wireless security and for extending the physical range of service to which a wireless user has access.

AirPort
An Apple brand wireless Ethernet network.

always on
A system that maintains a dedicated network connection is considered "always on."

ARP *see Address Resolution Protocol*

Asynchronous Transfer Mode (ATM)
A network technology based on transferring data in cells or packets of a fixed size. The cell used with ATM is relatively small compared to units used with older technologies. The small, constant cell size allows ATM equipment to transmit video, audio, and computer data over the same network, and ensures that no single type of data hogs the line.

ATM *see Asynchronous Transfer Mode*

B

back up
To copy files to a second medium (a disk, tape, cd, etc.) as a precaution in case the first medium fails.

binary digit
The smallest unit of information on a machine. The term was first used in 1946 by John Tukey, a leading statistician and adviser to five presidents. A single bit can hold only one of two values: 0 or 1. More meaningful information is obtained by combining consecutive bits into larger units.

bandwidth
(1) A range within a band of frequencies or wavelengths. (2) The amount of data that can be transmitted in a fixed amount of time. For digital devices, the bandwidth is usually expressed in bits per second (bps) or bytes per second. For analog devices, the bandwidth is expressed in cycles per second, or Hertz (Hz).

bits *see binary digit*

bits per second
Number of 1s and 0s (bits) traveling across a single point on a network each second.

Bluetooth
A short-range radio technology aimed at simplifying communications among Net devices and between devices and the Internet. It also aims to simplify data synchronization between Net devices and other computers. Products with Bluetooth technology must be qualified and pass interoperability testing by the Bluetooth Special Interest Group prior to release.

BOOTP *see bootstrap protocol*

bootstrap protocol
An Internet protocol that enables a diskless workstation to discover its own IP address, the IP address of a BOOTP server on the network, and a file to be loaded into memory to boot the machine. This enables the workstation to boot without requiring a hard or floppy disk drive. The protocol is defined by RFC 951.

Bps *see bits per second*

broadband
A type of data transmission in which a single medium (wire) can carry several channels at once. Cable TV, for example, uses broadband transmission. In contrast, baseband transmission allows only one signal at a time.

broadcast
To simultaneously send the same message to multiple recipients. Broadcasting is a useful feature in e-mail systems. It is also supported by some fax systems.

browser
A software application used to locate and display Web pages. The two most popular browsers are Netscape Navigator and Microsoft Internet Explorer. Both of these are graphical browsers, which means that they can display graphics as well as text. In addition, most modern browsers can present multimedia information, including sound and video, though they require plug-ins for some formats.

C

cat 5 *see category 5*

category 5
A multipair conductor, high-performance network cable. Category 5 (or cat 5) cable contains an even number of conductors with every pair of conductors twisted together for optimal data transmission.

CDMA *see Code Division Multiple Access*

CD-ROM *see Compact Disk Read-Only Memory*

coax *see coaxial cable*

coaxial cable
A type of wire that consists of a center wire surrounded by insulation and then a grounded shield of braided wire. The shield minimizes electrical and radio frequency interference.

Code Division Multiple Access (CDMA)
A digital cellular technology that uses spread-spectrum techniques. Unlike competing systems, such as GSM, that use TDMA, CDMA does not assign a specific frequency to each user. Instead, every channel uses the full available spectrum. Individual conversations are encoded with a pseudo-random digital sequence.

Compact Disk Read-Only Memory
A type of optical disk capable of storing large amounts of data—up to 1 GB, although the most common size is 650 MB. A single CD-ROM has the storage capacity of 700 floppy disks, enough memory to store about 300,000 text pages.

configuration
The way a system is set up, or the assortment of components that make up the system. Configuration can refer to either hardware or software, or the combination of both. For instance, a typical configuration for a PC consists of 32 MB main memory, a floppy drive, a hard disk, a modem, a CD-ROM drive, a VGA monitor, and the Windows operating system.

Control Panel
(1) A Macintosh utility that permits you to set many of the system parameters. For example, you can control the type of beeps the Mac makes and the sensitivity of the mouse. On older Macs (System 6 and earlier), control panels are called cdevs. ★(2) The Windows operating system has a Control Panel program that offers many of the same features as the Macintosh control panels.

crossover cables
Network cables with wires on one end of the cable reversed with respect to the other end. These cables are used to interconnect like devices such as PC to PC or hub to hub.

D

data
Stored digital information.

DHCP *see Dynamic Host Control Protocol*

Digital Subscriber Lines (DSL)
Broadband digital telephone line. DSL Technology transmits information (voice, video, and data) at fast speeds over existing copper telephone lines.

Direct Sequence Spread Spectrum (DSSS)
One of two types of spread spectrum radio, the other being frequency-hopping spread spectrum. DSSS is a transmission technology used in LAWN transmissions where a data signal at the sending station is combined with a higher data rate bit sequence, or chipping code, that divides the user data according to a spreading ratio. The chipping code is a redundant bit pattern for each bit that is transmitted, which increases the signal's resistance to interference. If one or more bits in the pattern are damaged during transmission, the original data can be recovered due to the redundancy of the transmission.

directories
1) On the World Wide Web, a directory is a subject guide, typically organized by major topics and subtopics. The best-known directory is the one at Yahoo (*www.yahoo.com*). Many other sites now use a Yahoo-like directory, including major portal sites. 2) In computer file systems, a directory is a named group of related files that are separated by the naming convention from other groups of files. 3) In computer networks, a directory is a collection of users, user passwords, and, usually, information about what network resources they can access.

DLC
The service provided by the Data Link layer of function defined in the Open Systems Interconnection (OSI) model for network communication. The Data Link layer is responsible for providing reliable data transfer across one physical link (or telecommunications path) within the network. Some of its primary functions include defining frames, performing error detection or ECC on those frames, and performing flow control (to prevent a fast sender from overwhelming a slow receiver). In LANs where connections are multipoint rather than point-to-point and require more line-sharing management, the Data Link layer is divided into two sublayers: the Logical Link Control layer and the Media Access Control (MAC) layer. The Logical Link Control layer protocol performs many of the same functions as the point-to-point data link control protocols described above. The MAC layer protocols support methods of sharing the line among a number of computers. Among the most widely used MAC protocols are ethernet (IEEE 802.3), token bus (IEEE 802.4), token ring (IEEE 802.5), and their derivatives.

DNS *see Domain Name System*

DNS servers

The server that translates human-readable domain names into an IP address. If a DNS server does not know or cannot translate a domain name into an IP address, it will ask another DNS server until it can find the answer.

domain

(1) In computing and telecommunication in general, a domain is a sphere of knowledge identified by a name. Typically, the knowledge is a collection of facts about some program entities or a number of network points or addresses. (2) On the Internet, a domain consists of a set of network addresses. This domain is organized in levels. The top level identifies geographic or purpose commonality (for example, the nation that the domain covers or a category such as "commercial"). The second level identifies a unique place within the top level domain and is, in fact, equivalent to a unique address on the Internet (an IP address). Lower levels of domain may also be used.

Domain Name System (DNS)

A hierarchical system for discovery of IP addresses from fully qualified domain names.

Domain Name Registrars

Organizations that maintain domain name registries; highest level of domain authority.

DSL *see Digital Subscriber Lines*

DSSS *see Direct Sequence Spread Spectrum*

DVD-ROM

Mass storage device allowing high density permanent storage similar to a CD-ROM.

Dynamic Host Control Protocol (DHCP)

A network protocol that allows computers on a network to be assigned IP addresses dynamically by a software program known as a DHCP server.

E

Electro-Magnetic Interference (EMI)

Spurious radio signals of varying frequencies that interrupt the electronic signal quality of a device. This interference normally affects wireless devices.

EMI *see Electro-Magnetic Interference*

ESSID *see Extended Service Set Identifier*

ethernet

A communications standard for network communications designed to eliminate network data collisions, thereby increasing network efficiency.

Extended Service Set Identifier (ESSID)

Alphanumeric code shared between wireless access point hardware and wireless Network Interface Cards (NICs).

F

FastHubs
Network hubs that operate at data transfer rates above 100 Mbps and faster.

FDM *see Frequency Division Multiplexing*

fiber optic cable
Glass and plastic cable over which laser light pulses travel. Laser light pulses over a fiber optic cable allow for greater data throughput than traditional copper wire.

firewall
Network device designed to act as a barrier between networks. Firewalls provide security, particularly between the public Internet and LANs.

firewire (IEEE 1394)
IEEE standard for high-speed serial communications between computers and computer peripherals. It is similar to USB.

FQDN *see Fully Qualified Domain Name*

frequency
Rate at which something occurs. In wireless networking, the rate at which the radio wave oscillates, usually measured in thousands of millions of cycles per second, a measure called Kilohertz (KHz) and Megahertz (MHz), respectively.

Frequency Division Multiplexing (FDM)
A communications scheme in which numerous signals are combined for transmission on a single communications line or channel. Each signal is assigned a different frequency (subchannel) within the main channel.

Frequency Shift Keying (FSK)
A modem converts the binary data from a computer to analog FSK signals for transmission over telephone lines, cables, fiber optic, or wireless media. The modem also converts incoming FSK signals to digital low and high states, which the computer can "understand."

FSK *see Frequency Shift Keying*

Fully Qualified Domain Name (FQDN)
An alias for an IP address that includes the computer host name, a network name, and a top-level domain such as COM, ORG, EDU and GOV.

G

gateway
A computer or device that provides routing services between networks.

Global Positioning Systems (GPS)
Devices that triangulate signals from several orbiting satellites to provide an accurate position (usually in longitude and latitude).

GPS *see Global Positioning Systems*

group
A group of computers on a network, sometimes called a workgroup. A group of computers can share network resources between computers.

Group Spéciale Mobile (GSM)
Group formed by European Conference of Post and Telecommunications Administrations in 1982 to develop a pan-European cellular phone system. GSM is how that cellular standard is known now.

H

hacker
Person who attempts to gain unauthorized access to computer systems and computer programs.

hardware
Physical device or devices that comprise a computer system. Hardware does not refer to stored programs. Those are known as firmware or software.

host
An individual computer on a network. Hosts are generally known on a network by a host name. Each host is recognized by an IP address.

harmonic distortion
Interference pattern found on the systems of commercial electric utility companies caused by an increase in switching power supplies connected to the power grid. In some cases the harmonic distortion is intense enough to cause damage to electronics receiving power from the utility.

HomePNA *see Home Phoneline Networking Alliance*

Home Phoneline Networking Alliance (HomePNA)
An association of networking companies working to create a unified phoneline networking standard.

Home Radio Frequency (HomeRF)
A standard developed by the HomeRF Working group to create a unified standard for interoperable wireless networking.

HomeRF *see Home Radio Frequency*

hub
A device that forms a common connection point for ethernet networks. Hubs generally form the center of networks configured in a star pattern. They are also known as network hubs.

I

IANA *see Internet Assigned Numbers Authority*

ICMP *see Internet Control Message Protocol*

ICS *see Internet Connection Sharing*

IEEE 802.11 *see Wi-Fi*

IEEE 1394 *see firewire*

IIS *see Internet Information Server*

Industry Standard Architecture (ISA)
The bus used in standard IBM-compatible PCs to provide power to add-in boards and communication between the add-in boards and the motherboard.

Infrared (IR)
Long wavelength light below the color spectrum visible to the human eye. This wavelength of light is used to send wireless light signals between computers, handhelds, palmtops, PDAs, and peripherals through an optional IR port. Limited networking is possible through the IR port.

interference
Radio signals that conflict with the integrity of other radio signals, such as those used in wireless networks. For example, a microwave oven may send out high-frequency radio waves that may interfere with networks using the same radio frequency.

Integrated Services Digital Network (ISDN)
ISDN is an early telephone company attempt at creating digital subscriber lines.

Internet
Global public ethernet data network originally known as ARPANET developed by researchers in the early 1970s that currently provides network communications to most of the planet, and soon to outer space.

Internet Assigned Numbers Authority (IANA)
Organization that acts as the central coordinating body for the Internet. IANA sets standards for such things as the distribution of IP addresses.

Internet Connection Sharing (ICS)
A scheme by which more than one computer can share a single Internet IP address and Internet connection to communicate over the Internet.

Internet Control Message Protocol
A protocol that uses datagrams to report errors in transmission between the host and the gateway.

Internet Information Server (IIS)
Microsoft Web server program.

Internet Protocol (IP)
The network software that delivers packets created by the Transmission Control Protocol program.

Internet Requests For Comments (Internet RFC)
A series of documents containing technical and organizational notes about the Internet. Memos in the RFC series discuss many aspects of computer networking, including protocols, procedures, programs, and concepts, as well as meeting notes, opinions, and sometimes humor. The RFCs were edited by Jon Postel from their inception in 1969 to his death in 1998.

Internet RFC *see Internet Requests For Comments*

Internet Service Provider (ISP)
Organization that provides Internet connectivity and Web hosting services.

IP *see Internet Protocol*

IR *see Infrared*

ISA *see Industry Standard Architecture*

ISDN *see Integrated Services Digital Network*

ISP *see Internet Service Provider*

K

Kbps
Kilobits per second. Transfer rate of bits across two points measured in thousands of bits (1s and 0s) per second.

L

LAN *see Local Area Network*

latency
Lag time or how long you have to wait for something to happen. On a network, it is the time it takes for a packet to reach its destination.

LAWN
A local area wireless network.

line of site
When one device is able to send radio signals directly to another device completely unobstructed or without requiring the radio signal to bounce, bend or curve; a direct path between two points.

Local Area Network (LAN)
A network of computers located in a single location, such as your home.

M

MAC *see Media Access Control*

Mbps
Megabits per second, a data transfer rate measured in millions of bits per second. See Kbps.

Media Access Control (MAC)
Special coded hardware address.

modem
A device that converts digital data into sound for transmission across a telephone system.

MS-DOS
Microsoft Disk Operating System; an early text-based operating system for personal computers.

N

NAT *see Network Address Translation*

NetBEUI *see Network BIOS Enhanced User Interface*

network
Two or more computers interconnected in such that data can be communicated between them using a networking protocol such as TCP/IP.

network adapter *see Network Interface Card*

Network Address Translation (NAT)
The primary function of many routers. Every packet passing through a gateway is read and when NAT is enabled, the control information in the header is changed so that it appears as though the packet was sent from the gateway machine. A table is maintained on the gateway, logging each outbound packet. When a response returns, NAT can refer to the table to determine which computer originally sent the packet so it may be routed back to the right computer.

Network BIOS Enhanced User Interface (NetBEUI)
A protocol that allows PCs to communicate with one another over a network.

network card *see Network Interface Card*

Network Interface Card (NIC)
A computer expansion card that provides network connectivity, either wired or wireless. The NIC provides low-level network communications functionality.

Network Neighborhood
Part of the Windows operating system; a visual representation of network connections between computers allowing you to share and use shared resources.

NIC *see Network Interface Card*

O

operating system
The software that provides basic file system and peripheral communications. Operating systems are required on all programmable computers. Examples of operating systems include Windows, MacOS, Unix, and Linux.

P

packets
Organization of data into small groups designed to travel over a network, and be reconstructed in the proper order at the receiving end. Packets are individually addressed and routed to their destination. Portions of a data stream may take different paths to the target destination.

PAN *see Personal Area Network*

parallel port
Computer communications port that sends data in parallel instead of in a stream as in a serial port. Parallel ports are also called printer ports because in the past this was their primary purpose. In fact, they usually carry the LPT (Line Printer Terminal) port designation. Computers can have more than one LPT port and carry the numbers LPT1, LPT2, and so on.

PC *see Personal Computer*

PCI *see Peripheral Component Interconnect*

PCMCIA *see Personal Computer Memory Card International Association*

PDA *see Personal Digital Assistant*

Peripheral Component Interconnect (PCI)
A 32-bit expansion bus for communication between expansion cards and computer motherboards. PCI is a newer and faster bus compared to ISA.

peripheral devices
Devices connected to a computer that are not considered to be integral. Integral devices are the CPU, keyboard, and monitor. Examples of peripheral devices are printers and scanners.

permissions
Security setting that provides varying levels of access to the file or file system by end users or programs.

Personal Area Network (PAN)
A network of computers, peripherals, and devices carried on one's person.

Personal Computer (PC)
A class of computers normally sold as devices meant to be owned and used by an individual person. They were dubbed personal computers by IBM with the invention of the IBM PC. This was the first class of computers considered affordable in the consumer marketplace.

Personal Computer Memory Card International Association (PCMCIA)
This trade association is responsible for establishing the standard for small expansion cards used largely in portable computers. The standard bears the acronym of the association as its name.

Personal Digital Assistant (PDA)
A small handheld device that usually has software for managing contacts and maintaining a calendar, and is often equipped with IR networking capability for synchronizing with a desktop PC.

phoneline network
A mechanism for creating a network of computers using traditional telephone lines running throughout your home or office.

Ping
A program designed to test the accessibility of a remote computer by sending ICMP packets and expecting them to be echoed back.

Plain Old Telephone Service (POTS)
The designation given to the standard, analog telephone service.

PoE *see Power over Ethernet*

POTS *see Plain Old Telephone Service*

ports
This term can have several meanings. When referred to in reference to networking, it usually refers to a numbering system for packet delivery by which packets are sent to programs registered to receive data bearing a particular port number. Ports can also refer to the female RJ45 plugs in a network hub.

Power over Ethernet (PoE)
A mechanism for sending 5V dc over an ethernet cable to power devices remotely.

powerline network
A means of networking computers by sending the network data over the power lines in your home or office. These network devices plug into the 110V ac wall sockets.

profile
Profiles are configuration files that maintain a user's preferences.

protocols
The languages machines use to communicate with one another.

proxy
A computer or software program that acts as a secure gateway between two networks.

Q

QoS *see Quality of Service*

Quality of Service (QoS)
The ability of some networks to reserve bandwidth for particular applications based on their expected bandwidth requirements. When bandwidth is reserved, the quality of the data signal can be guaranteed. When bandwidth is not reserved, data travels in a first-come, first-served basis and data throughput cannot be guaranteed.

R

RFC *see Internet Request For Comments*

RJ11
Modular phone jack and plug used in most modern phone systems. RJ11 jacks and plugs are designed to accommodate four-conductor cable.

RJ45
Modular jack and plug used in most ethernet networks. RJ45 appear similar to RJ11 jacks and plugs except they are larger and can accommodate eight conductors.

routers
Devices with the capability of redirecting network traffic based on IP addresses and netmasks.

S

server
A software program that waits on requests sent from software client programs and performs services based on the client request. Computers that run server software are also known generically as servers or can be referred to by the service they provide (for example, Web server).

Shared Wireless Access Protocol (SWAP)
HomeRF specification for wireless communications.

Shielded Twisted Pair (STP)
A cable type containing any even number of conductors in which pairs of conductors are twisted together for greater data delivery efficiency, and surrounded by a metallic interference shield. The shield is usually either foil or a metal braid.

SOCKS
A firewall communications protocol that allows programs from one network to communicate through a firewall to a program on another network.

software
Programs designed to run on a computer, loaded at run time from a temporary data storage medium. This is different from firmware, which are software programs stored in permanent or semipermanent hardware storage (on chips).

spam
Unsolicited messages delivered over a public data network, usually through e-mail and instant messenger programs.

STP *see Shielded Twisted Pair*

streaming media
Multimedia files that are viewed or played while the data is still being transferred from

the source. Historically, large multimedia files had to be completely downloaded and saved before viewing or listening to their contents. Streaming media enabled nearly instant gratification on even slower network connections.

subnet mask
An addressing mechanism for packet delivery over ethernet networks. They appear like IP addresses in dotted quad format but provide different functionality.

SWAP *see Share Wireles Access Protocol*

T

TCP *see Transmission Control Protocol*

TCP/IP *see Transmission Control Protocol/Internet Protocol*

terminal server
A computer with the ability to provide functionality by allowing computers to run software remotely that is installed on the terminal server.

topology
The configuration of a network. There are three basic network topologies: star, daisy chain, and token ring.

traffic
Data traveling over a network.

Transmission Control Protocol (TCP)
Network software that breaks data into packets and then hands them off to the Internet Protocol (IP) for transmission across a TCP/IP network.

Transmission Control Protocol / Internet Protocol (TCP/IP)
The suite of network protocols used on most networks and on the Internet.

Trojan horse
A malicious imposter program that does not replicate or deliver itself. It will appear as though it is a legitimate program until it has been executed. Trojan horse programs are often used by hackers to gain unauthorized access to compromised computer systems.

Troubleshooting
The method followed by someone attempting to find the source of a failure or breakdown. It is performed until it is deemed necessary to call customer support.

U

UDP *see User Datagram Protocol*

Uninterruptible Power Supply (UPS)
A battery equipped with an inverter that converts 12V dc to 120V ac to provide temporary power to computer systems in the event of a power failure.

Universal Plug and Play
The software system that allows newly installed hardware to automatically be recognized by the computer and initiates the installation of associated driver software.

Universal Serial Bus (USB)
A high-speed serial communication system that allows devices to be daisy-chained together. The USB port is rapidly replacing the traditional nine-pin serial port. Modern computers are generally equipped with one or more USB ports. This port can provide networking capability or can be used to connect removable NICs.

Unshielded Twisted Pair (UTP)
Network cables containing an even number of conductors in which every pair of conductors is twisted together to increase data transfer efficiency. This cable is covered with a plastic insulator. It provides minimal data-interference protection.

UPNP
A movement to provide plug and play capability to any device that may be connected to a network, including consumer electronics. See also Universal Plug and Play.

UPS *see Uninterruptible Power Supply*

UTP *see Unshielded Twisted Pair*

USB *see Universal Serial Bus*

user
Anyone using a computer or peripheral device.

User Datagram Protocol (UDP)
A means of sending data packets (datagrams) across a network without establishing a connection between two programs. When data is sent, there is no acknowledgment of its receipt. UDP is used when broadcasting data to large numbers of computers.

V

virtual drive
An alias for either a shared network drive or an area of computer memory that appears like a drive. Each is recognized by the computer operating system as a drive and given a drive letter as though it were a disk-based drive.

Virtual Private Network (VPN)
A network of computers that is spread out over a wide area network such as the Internet, but mimics a LAN. VPNs allow computers to maintain secure communication between other computers connected to the virtual private network as though they were not a part of the wide area network.

Virtual Reality (VR)
The ability to immerse yourself in a visual 3-D computer-generated environment either through the use of a head-mounted display or a room with encircling large displays. Virtual reality, through the use of special user input devices such as a data glove, allow the user to interact with the objects in the computer environment as though they were real objects. Some user input devices even have tactile feedback, making the experience of touching virtual objects even more lifelike.

virus
Malicious program that replicates and executes itself. Viruses are spread by attaching themselves to host files.

VPN *see Virtual Private Network*

VR *see Virtual Reality*

W

Web *see World Wide Web*

Whitecap
The communication protocol for devices that incorporate ShareWave brand technology.

Wi-Fi (802.11, 802.11a, 802.11b)
Wireless networking protocol.

wireless
Data transfer using radio waves. Data transfer can be both digital and analog. Home networks use digital transfer while amateur radios use packet radio modems to transfer data without wires.

Wizard
A software program, or part of a software program, that provides step-by-step assistance during installation and configuration functions.

workgroup
A named group of computers on a network. Computers in a workgroup can easily share files and peripherals with each other. Security can also be defined at the workgroup level.

World Wide Web
A network client-server program that allows documents to be requested by client programs and delivered by server programs using the HTTP (Hypertext Transport Protocol). Web documents, known as pages, are normally displayed by the client program (browser) in a graphical environment.

worms
A type of virus that does not attach itself to a host file. Instead, a worm uses a host file in such a way that the entire host file must be considered to be the worm.

www   *see World Wide Web*

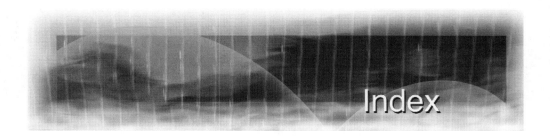

Index

1000baseT, 32
100baseT, 26–27
  cables for, 32
  hubs, 47
  network cards, 43
  troubleshooting, 180
10baseT, 25–26
  cables for, 32
  hubs, 47
  network cards, 43
  troubleshooting, 180
3Com, 42
802.11 standard, 12, 202
802.11a standard, 15–16
802.11b standard, 14–16
802.11e standard, 15

A

Abramson, Norman, 24
ac ground wire, 20
access points, 84–85
acoustic sensors, 200
ActionLink USB Cable Room-to-Room
    Starter kit, 28
ActionTec, 28
Active Directory, 137
adapters, 102
Address Resolution Protocol (ARP), 150
administrators, 136
ADSL modems, 53

Advanced Research Project Agency
    Network (ARPANet), 4
air conditioning systems, 198
AirPort, 15
ALOHANET, 11, 24
AND operation, 92–93
AnyPoint phoneline network, 50
AOL Instant Messenger, 171
Apple Computer, 15, 29
Apple Filing Protocol, 129
AppleTalk network, 3, 129–130
application sharing, 4
ARP (Address Resolution Protocol), 150
ARPANet (Advanced Research Project
  Agency Network), 4
ATM (Asynchronous Transfer Mode), 32
audio systems, 202
authentication attempts, 86
automobiles, 202–203

B

backup operators, 136
backups, 171–172
  hard drives, 174
  hot swappable drives, 175
  Internet backup services, 173–174
  Jaz disks, 173
  tape drives, 172
  writeable CD-ROMs, 172–173
  writeable DVD-ROMs, 173

backups *(continued)*
  Zip disks, 173
  See also drives
bandwidth, 10, 82, 164
baseband, 25
binary numbers, 91
BIOS (Basic Input Output System), 101
biosensors, 199
.biz, 105
blackouts, 80
Bluetooth, 18–20
Bluetooth, Harald, 18
Boolean arithmetic, 92
bootp, 152
broadband connections, 82, 146
broadband routers, 157
brownouts, 80
buffer overflow, 167–168

C

cable Internet, 22
cable modems, 146
  and access points, 84
  crossover cables for, 33
  in phoneline networks, 22
  plugging into network hubs, 47
  as routers, 146–147
cables, 32
  Category 3, 33
  Category 4, 33
  Category 5, 33, 35
  checking, 38
  crossover, 33–34
  distances, 72
  fiber optic, 81–82
  hidden installation of, 63–65
  installing, 69–73
  labeling, 73
  making own, 34–37
  network, 32–33
  outdoor wiring, 73–75

troubleshooting, 178–179
  in weatherproof conduits, 73
cabling tools, 63–64, 66–69
caching, 128
cameras, 21
car audio systems, 202
Category 3 cable, 33
Category 4 cable, 33
Category 5 cable, 22, 33, 35
Cayman Systems, 53
CD-R drives, 133
CD-ROM burners, 172–173
CD-ROM drives, 133
CD-ROMs, 172–173
CD-RW drives, 133
CD Writers, 172–173
CDMA phone system, 202
Cisco, 197
Class A networks, 94, 148
Class B networks, 94, 148
Class C networks, 93–94, 148
Class D networks, 148
Class E networks, 148
Classic File Sharing, 126–128
Client for Microsoft Networks, 100–101
client software, 102
clients, 165
climate-control systems, 198
coaxial cables, 32
Code Red virus, 169
.com, 105
Combo Card, 43, 50
communication, 2
computer networks. *See* networks
computers
  attaching printers to, 111
  in automobiles, 203
  configuring for network printing,
      114–118
  distance between hubs and, 72
  in ethernet networks, 24

as firewalls, 157
handwriting recognition in, 207
infection with viruses, 203
IP addresses of, 146
mainframe, 2–3
notebook computers, 205–207
opening, 39–42
packet radio network of, 11
pen tablets, 205–207
in phoneline networks, 52
power supplies, 80
as proxy servers, 155–156
remote connection to, 137–140
sharing of, 133–136
subnet masks, 92
voice recognition in, 207
conduits, 73
connections, 178–179
and network configurations, 181
slow or intermittent, 190–191
testing, 185–187
tracing the paths of, 187–189
connectors, 34–35
copper wire, 81
cordless telephones, 15
Create Shared Folder Wizard, 124
credit card numbers, 165, 167
crimpers, 34, 63
crossover cables, 33–34
crossover ports, 48–49

D

D-Link, 42, 154
daisy-chain topology, 28, 60
data ports, 48–49
data speeds
9.6-115.2 Kbps, 17
115 Kbps, 77
360 Kbps, 77
721 Kbps, 18
1 Mbps, 20, 50

2 Mbps, 77
4 Mbps, 28
10 Mbps, 20, 22, 25, 33, 50
11 Mbps, 14, 16
14 Mbps, 77
16 Mbps, 33
54 Mbps, 15–16
100 Mbps, 25–26, 33
400 Mbps, 29
for ports, 77
for twisted-pair cables, 33
data storage
hard drives, 174
hot swappable drives, 175
Internet backup services, 173–174
Jaz disks, 173
tape drives, 172
writeable CD-ROMs, 172–173
writeable DVD-ROMs, 173
Zip disks, 173
datagrams, 185
dead spots, 85
debugger users, 137
default gateways, 94–95, 183
denial-of-service attacks, 168
Denmark, 18
Department of Defense (DoD), 4
Department of Education, 4
desktop themes, 133
Device Manager, 191–192
DHCP (Dynamic Host Control Protocol),
88, 91
DHCP servers, 91, 151
in hardware devices, 154
setting up, 152–154
using at homes, 151
See also IP addresses
dial tone, 52
Digital Equipment, 3
Digital Marketplace Inc., 107
Digital Powerline technology, 23

Direct Sequence Spread Spectrum (DSSS), 14
directories. *See* folders
disk space, 165–166
Display tab, 140
DNS servers, 105–107, 183
DNS suffix, 183
DoD (Department of Defense), 4
domain name registrars, 106
domain names, 104–106
door/window sensors, 200
dotted decimal notation, 91–92
dotted quad notation, 91–92
downloading, 164
DPL 1000, 23
drill motors, 63
drills, 66
drivers
    for network cards, 191–193
    for printers, 119–120
    troubleshooting, 191–193
drives
    hard drives, 174
    hot swappable drives, 175
    Jaz disks, 173
    mapping, 132–133
    removable, 173
    sharing, 120–121
    tape drives, 172
    Zip drives, 173
    See also backups
DSL modems, 146
    and access points, 84
    crossover cables for, 33
    in phoneline networks, 22
    plugging into network hubs, 47
    as routers, 146–147
DSSS (Direct Sequence Spread Spectrum), 14
dual-speed hubs, 47
dumb terminals, 2–3
DVD players, 200
DVD-ROM drives, 133, 173

Dynamic Host Control Protocol (DHCP), 88, 91
dynamic IP addresses, 88, 151
dynamic packet inspection, 157

E

e-mail, 165
.edu, 105
electric jigsaw, 63
electric motors, 190
electric power, 80
electrical noise, 81
electromagnetic interference (EMI), 32
EMI (electromagnetic interference), 32
Ericsson, 18–19
ESSID (Extended Service Set Identifier), 104
ethernet, 24–25
    100baseT, 26–27
    10baseT, 25–26
    cables for, 32–33
    hubs, 46
    invention of, 3
    latency, 78
    network interface cards, 43–46
    See also networks; LANs
        (local area networks)
Experience tab, 141
Extended Service Set Identifier (ESSID), 104
extension cords, 78
EZ-Link Instant Network, 28

F

faceplates, 65
fasteners, 67
FastHub, 72
fault-protected PoE injectors, 55
fax machines, 18
FDM (Frequency Division Multiplexing), 21
fiber networks, 81–82
fiber optic cables, 32, 81–82

File and Printer Sharing service, 100–101
file sharing, 4, 100–101
    classic, 126–128
    on Macintosh computers, 129–131
    in phoneline networks, 22
    simple, 123–126
    See also network sharing
filters, 22, 80–81
fire protection systems, 196
FireNet, 29
firewalls, 156, 170–171
    hardware, 157–158
    software, 156–157
Firewire, 29–30
fish tape, 63
five-plug multiline extension cords, 79
floods, 81
floppy disks, 169
folders, 120–121
    accessing, 129
    ownership of, 133
    sharing of
        on Macintosh computers, 131
        on Windows 95, 98 and ME, 121–122
    subfolders for, 171
four-pair cable pinout, 36
FQDN (Fully Qualified Domain Name),
        105, 152
French Optical Telegraph Network, 2
Frequency Division Multiplexing
        (FDM), 21
FSK (Frequency Shift Keying (FSK), 23
Fujitsu E Series notebook computers,
        205–206
Fujitsu Stylistic 3500R Pen tablet, 205–206
Fujitsu Stylistic LT P-600F Pen table,
        205–206
full control access, 128
Fully Qualified Domain Name (FQDN),
        105, 152
Furman Sound, 81

G

gadgets, 199–200
game consoles, 201
Gamecube, 201
gateways, 94–95
General tab, 140
GET request, 150
Global Positioning System (GPS), 202
GoDaddy.com, 106
.gov, 105
GPS (Global Positioning System), 202
GRD-267DTV refrigerator, 197–198
groups, 136–137
GSM phone system, 202
Guest account, 123–124
guests, 136

H

H.26L video standard, 200
hackers, 85, 166–168
ham radio, 11
handwriting recognition, 207
hard drives, 174
    backing up, 174
    hot swappable, 175
    mapping, 132–133
    organizing, 171
    sharing of, 3, 120–121, 171
    See also drives
harmonic distortion, 80–81
Hawaii, 11, 24
HelpServicesGroup, 137
HFC (hybrid fiber-coaxial cable), 82
Hi-Fi (High-Fidelity) stereos, 14
home automation systems, 196–200
home education systems, 196
home entertainment systems, 196
home game consoles, 201
home networks, 4
    applications, 196

home networks *(continued)*
    automobiles, 202–203
home automation systems, 197–200
    home game consoles, 201
    video systems, 200
    virtual reality, 203–204
    wireless roaming, 202
    bandwidth requirements, 10
    default gateways, 94–95
    DHCP servers, 151
    integrating electronic devices in, 196
    IP addresses, 89
    power supplies, 79–81
    protecting, 165, 166
    requirements in, 5–6
    threats to security of, 166–169
    training on, 164
    troubleshooting, 178
        cables, 178–179
        configuration troubles, 181
        connections, 185–187
        hardware, 180
        IP conflicts, 189
        network cards, 191–193
        Network Neighborhood, 189–190
        wireless connections, 190–191
    types of, 11
    using, 6–7
    wired, 20
        ethernet, 24–25
        Firewire, 29–30
        phone lines, 20–23
        power lines in, 23–24
        USB (Universal Serial Bus), 27–29
    wireless, 11, 202
        Bluetooth, 18–20
    HomeRF (Home Radio Frequency),
        12–14
        IR (infrared), 17–18
        Wi-Fi (Wireless Fidelity), 14–17
home office systems, 196

Home Phoneline Networking Alliance
    (HomePNA), 20–23
Home Radio Frequency (HomeRF),
    12–14, 53–54
home security systems, 199
home video systems, 200
HomeFree phoneline network, 50
Homeline USB-to-phoneline adapters, 76
HomeLink phoneline network, 50
HomePNA (Home Phoneline Networking
    Alliance), 20–23
HomeRF (Home Radio Frequency),
    12–14, 53–54
hops, 187
host addresses, 92
host names, 183
hot swappable drives, 175
hubs, 46
    100baseT, 47
    10baseT, 47
    connecting, 49–50
    distance between computers and, 72
    in network layouts, 73
    selecting, 48–49
    wired, 46–47
    See also ports
hybrid fiber-coaxial cable (HFC), 82

I

IANA (Internet Assigned Numbers
    Authority), 88
IBM, 18
iBook computers, 15
ICQ, 171
ICS (Internet Connection Sharing), 149, 158
    installing on Windows 2000, 160
    installing on Windows 98/ME, 158–160
ID tag tie wraps, 68
IEEE 1394, 29
IIS (Internet Information Services), 139
iMac computers, 15

Industry Standard Architecture (ISA), 39–42
.info, 105
infrared (IR) wireless networks, 17–18
Initial parallel adapter, 77
Initial Power Packet, 75
injectors, 55–56
installing
    ICS (Internet Connection Sharing)
        on Windows 2000, 160
        on Windows 98/ME, 158–160
    NetBEUI (NetBios Extended User
            Interface), 189–190
    network components, 102–103
    printers, 111
instant messaging software, 167, 171
Intel, 3, 12, 18
Intellon network, 75
Intellum card, 77
interference, 85
Internet
    dedicated connections to, 146
    filtering access to, 157
    foundation of, 4
    and hacking, 167
    sharing access to, 4
    wireless, 15
Internet Assigned Numbers Authority
            (IANA), 88
Internet backup services, 173–174
Internet cafes, 15
Internet Connection Sharing. *See* ICS
Internet Explorer, 133
Internet Information Services (IIS), 139
Internet Protocol (IP), 88
Internet radio, 13
Internet-ready refrigerators, 197–198
Internet RFC 1878 standard, 92
Internet RFC 2734 standard, 29
Iomega, 173
IP addresses, 88
    of computers, 146
    configuration information, 181–183

conflicts in, 189
and dedicated Internet connections, 146
and DNS servers, 106–107
and domain names, 104–106
dynamic, 88, 151
local, 89–90
and Macintosh computers, 99–100
managing with DHCP servers, 151
multiple ISP-assigned, 89
of network cards, 156
and network classes, 94, 148
of routers, 148–149
static, 88, 90, 151
structure of, 91–92
subnet masks, 92–94
viewing
    in Windows 95/98/ME, 95–96
    in Windows NT/2000, 96–97
    in Windows XP, 97–99, 182–183
and Windows operating systems, 95–99
IP (Internet Protocol), 88
IP over IEEE 1394 standard, 29
IP routing, 183
IPConfig utility, 182–183
IPNet Monitor, 78
ISA (Industry Standard Architecture), 34–42
ISPs (Internet Service Providers), 88, 146

J

Jaz disks, 173

K

keyhole saw, 63

L

language, 2
LANs (local area networks), 3–4
    hubs, 47
    wireless, 11, 53
    See also networks; ethernet

laptops, 22, 34, 39
laser, 81
laser printers, 3, 24
latency, 78
LCDs (liquid crystal displays), 198, 202
LG Electronics Inc., 197–199
lightning, 80
line noise, 76–78
link lights, 179–180
Linksys, 42, 154
Linksys Etherfast 10/100 5-Port Workgroup
      Switch, 47
Linksys Etherfast Cable/DSL router, 147–148
liquid crystal displays (LCDs), 198, 202
local area networks. *See* LANs
Local Connection Properties window, 103
local IP addresses, 89, 146
Local Resources tab, 140
Lockdown Trojan protection software, 169
Lucent Technologies, 15

M

MAC (Media Access Control), 149, 183
Mac OS 8.5 operating system, 28
Mac OS 9 operating system, 129
Macintosh computers, 3
      file sharing on, 129–131
      and IP addresses, 99–100
      in phoneline networks, 21
      Wi-Fi (Wireless Fidelity) for, 15
      See also computers
magnetic tapes, 172
mainframe computers, 2–3, 101
Management and Monitoring Tools, 132
mapping network drives, 132–133
markers, 63
McAfee, 169
Media Access Control (MAC), 149, 183
Metcalf, Robert, 3, 24
microwave bands, 54
microwave ovens, 15, 190, 198

Mitnick, Kevin, 167
Mobile DHCP Service, 154–155
modems, 28, 146
motherboards, 39–41
motion sensors, 199
MP3 music files, 13, 202–203
MPEG-4 video standard, 200
MSN Messenger, 142–143
multi-line jacks, 78
multi-plug devices, 78
multicasting, 148
multiple IP addresses, 89
multipoint injectors, 56
Muus, Mike, 185

N

NAT (Network Address Table), 95
NAT (Network Address Translation), 150
NetBEUI (NetBios Extended User
      Interface), 100–102, 189–190
NetBIOS, 101
Netgear, 154
Netgear Cable/DSL Firewall Router,
      154–155
Netstat utility program, 184
network adapters, 29, 39
Network Address Table (NAT), 95
Network Address Translation (NAT), 150
network backups, 171–172
      hard drives, 174
      hot swappable drives, 175
      Internet backup services, 173–174
      Jaz disks, 173
      tape drives, 172
      writeable CD-ROMs, 172–173
      writeable DVD-ROMs, 172–173
      Zip disks, 173
network-based gaming, 4
network cables, 62
      distances, 72
      hidden installation of, 63–65

installing, 69–73
labeling, 73
outdoor wiring, 73–75
troubleshooting, 178–179
types of, 32–33
in weatherproof conduits, 73
See also cables
network cards, 39
assigning IP addresses to, 156
link lights, 180
troubleshooting, 179–180, 191–193
wireless, 83–84
See also NIC (Network Interface Card)
network classes, 94, 148
network collisions, 24
network components, 100–102
adding, 132
installing, 102–103
network configuration operators, 136
network gaming, 4, 22, 201
network hubs. *See* hubs
Network Interface Card. *See* NIC
network management, 164
disk space, 165–166
security, 166
training on, 164
Network Neighborhood, 131–132
accessing shared folders in, 129
troubleshooting, 189–190
Network Places, 129
network printers, 111
naming, 118–119
Windows 2000/XP, 115–118
Windows 95/98/ME, 114–115
network security, 166
backups in, 171–172
hard drives, 174
hot swappable drives, 175
Jaz disks, 173
tape drives, 172
third-party Internet backup, 173–174

writeable CD-ROMs, 172–173
writeable DVD-ROMs, 173
Zip disks, 173
preventing losses in, 170
threats to, 166–167
hackers, 167–168
Trojans, 169
viruses, 168–169
worms, 169
Network Services, 132
network sharing, 4
of computers, 133–136
of disks, 131
of files, 100–101, 120–121
on Macintosh, 129–130
on Windows XP, 123–128
of folders
on Macintosh, 131
on Windows/95/98/ME, 121–122
of printers, 100–101
networked clocks, 13
networked writing pads, 13
networking, 2–3, 178
networks
background, 2–3
backups in, 171–172
hard drives, 174
hot swappable drives, 175
Jaz disks, 173
tape drives, 172
third-party Internet backup, 173–174
writeable CD-ROMs, 172–173
writeable DVD-ROMs, 173
Zip disks, 173
bandwidth requirements, 10
classes, 94, 148
and communication, 2
components, 100–102
default gateways, 94–95
home networks, 4–7
hubs, 46

networks *(continued)*
    IP addresses, 89
    latency, 78
    mapping drives on, 132–133
    origin of, 2
    outdoor wiring, 73–75
    planning the layout of, 59
    power supplies, 79–81
    preventing losses in, 170–171
    protecting, 165
    reducing traffic on, 155
    setups, 100–102
    sharing printers on, 110–111
    threats to security of, 166–169
    topologies, 59–60
    troubleshooting, 178
        cables, 178–179
        configuration troubles, 181
        connections, 178–179, 185–187
        hardware, 180
        IP conflicts, 189
        network cards, 191–193
        Network Neighborhood, 189–190
        wireless connections, 190–191
    types of, 11
    wired, 20
        ethernet, 24–25
        Firewire, 29–30
        home phone lines, 20–23
        power lines in, 23–24
        USB (Universal Serial Bus), 27–29
    wireless, 11, 18–20
        HomeRF (Home Radio Frequency),
            12–14
        IR (infrared), 17–18
        Wi-Fi (Wireless Fidelity), 14–17
New Share button, 128
NIC (Network Interface Card), 39
    buying, 42
    installing, 43–46, 102
    selecting, 43–44

    troubleshooting, 179–180, 191–193
    for wireless networks, 83–84
    See also network cards
Nimda virus, 169
Nintendo, 201
node types, 183
Nokia, 18
Nortel, 23
Norton Antivirus, 169
notebook computers, 205–207
Novell, 3
NTII, 203

O

octets, 91
OnStar global positioning system, 202
outdoor wiring, 73–75

P

packet filters, 157
packet radio, 11
PANs (Personal Area Networks), 12–14, 18
parallel adapters, 77
parallel ports, 50–51
    maximum speed for, 77
    as printer ports, 111
passive PoE injectors, 55
passive taps, 55–56
passwords, 131, 167
PCs (personal computers), 2–3
    in automobiles, 203
    number of homes with, 4
    opening, 39–42
    in phoneline networks, 21
    See also computers
PCI cards, 50–51, 76
PCI (Peripheral Component Interconnect),
    39–42
PCMCIA cards, 34, 39
    in access-point equipment, 85
    in Wi-Fi networks, 14
peer-to-peer connections, 148
pen tablets, 205–207

Peripheral Component Interconnect (PCI), 39–42
permissions, 128
Personal Area Network (PAN), 12–14
Philips head screws, 40
phone jacks, 20–21, 34, 52
phoneline networks, 20–23
    adapters for, 76
    connections, 50–52
    data speed, 77
    equipment placement in, 75–76
    extending, 78–79
    filters for, 80–81
    general connection information, 52
    latency, 78
    line noise, 76–78
    network cards for, 76
    parallel port connection, 51
    PCI card connection, 51
    power supplies, 79–80
    USB port connection, 51
    See also networks; home networks
physical address, 149, 183
Ping, 78, 185–187
Plain Old Telephone Service (POTS), 21
Playstation 2, 201
pocket computers, 18
PoE injectors, 55–56
PoE (Power over Ethernet), 55–56
pool pumps, 190
port scanners, 165
ports, 48–49
    crossover ports, 48–49
    and firewalls, 157, 171
    for Internet applications, 165
    numbers, 165
    parallel, 50–51
printer, 111
    for remote connections, 139
    serial, 27–28
    USB (Universal Serial Bus), 27–29

    See also hubs
POTS (Plain Old Telephone Service), 21
power failures, 80
power isolation transformers, 81
Power Mac G4 computers, 15
power on/off sensors, 200
Power over Ethernet (PoE), 55–56
power supplies, 79–80
power surges, 80
power users, 136
PowerBook G4 computers, 15
powerline networks, 23–24
    data speed, 77
    equipment placement in, 75–76
    extending, 78–79
    filters for, 80–81
    latency, 78
    line noise, 76–78
    power supplies, 79–80
    and surge protectors, 79
    See also home networks; networks
primary DNS suffix, 183
print servers, 111–112
    Windows 2000/XP, 113–114
    Windows 95/98/ME, 112
printers, 21
    attaching to computers, 111
    configuring for network sharing, 111
    drivers, 119–120
    naming, 118–119
    network, 111
    in phoneline networks, 21
    sharing of, 2–3, 100–101, 110–111
private internets, 89–90
programmers, 3
protocols, 88, 102
Proxim, 12, 15
proxy servers, 146, 155–156
PS2 Broadband, 201

Q

Quality of Service (QoS), 15

R

radio broadcasting equipment, 190
Radio Shack, 34, 52
radio signals, 60
radio waves, 11
read-only access, 128
refrigerators, 197–198
registered users, 130–131
regulated taps, 55–56
Remote Assistant, 141–143
Remote Desktop Connection, 141
remote desktop users, 137
Remote Desktop Web Connection, 139
replicators, 137
Request Timed Out message, 187
residential gateways, 196–197
rewriteable CD-ROMs, 172–173
RFC 1878 standard, 92
RFC 1918 standard, 89
ring topology, 32, 60
RJ11 telephone jacks, 34
RJ45 connectors, 34, 63, 73
roaming, 155, 202
root folders, 120
routers, 146–150
    broadband, 157
as firewalls, 157
    IP addresses of, 148–149
    proxy server programs as, 156

S

safe deposit boxes, 174
scanners, 21
security systems, 196, 199
sensors, 199–200

serial ports, 27–28
    maximum speed for, 77
    as printer ports, 111
Server Scope Properties window, 152
servers, 165
services, 102
set top boxes, 22, 196
Share Wireless Access Protocol (SWAP), 12
shared Internet access, 4
ShareWave, 15
sharing
    computers, 133–136
    disks, 131
    files, 100–101
        on Macintosh, 129–130
        on Windows XP, 123–128
    folders, 120–121
        on Macintosh, 131
        on Windows/95/98/ME, 121–122
    hard drives, 3, 120–121, 171
    printers, 100–101, 110–111
SimpleDevices, 12
SimpleFi home stereo, 12–13
single-point injectors, 56
social engineering, 167
social security numbers, 167
Sony Corp., 201
spa pumps, 190
spam, 166
splitters, 22, 52, 78–79
staple guns, 63, 67
staples, 67–69
star topology, 28, 60
Starbucks, 15
stateful packet inspection, 157
static IP addresses, 88, 90, 151
stations, 24
streaming media, 12
subfolders, 171

subnet masks, 92–94, 183
surge protectors, 52, 80
Sustainable Networks, 78
SWAP (Share Wireless Access Protocol), 12

T

tape drives, 172
tape measure, 63
taps, 55–56
TCP/IP (Transmission Control
Protocol/Internet Protocol), 3–4, 100–101
TCP (Transmission Control Protocol), 165
telegraphs, 2
telephones, 2, 196
    extension plugs for, 78
    in networking, 20–23
    wireless, 190
television sets, 196
temperature sensors, 200
terminal servers, 140
Terminal Services, 140
third-party Internet backup services, 173–174
tie wraps, 67–68
tone generators, 38, 180–181
tone probes, 38, 180–181
top-level domain names, 105
topologies, 59–60
Toshiba, 18
Traceroute utility, 187–189
Transmission Control Protocol (TCP), 165
transportation systems, 196
Trojans, 165, 169
troubleshooting, 178
    configuration troubles, 181
    connections, 178–179, 185–187
    device drivers, 191–193
    with Device Manager, 191–193
    IP conflicts, 189
    network cards, 191–193

Network Neighborhood, 189–190
    tools for, 180
    wireless connections, 190–191
twisted-pair cables, 32–33

U

U-shaped staples, 67
UDP (User Datagram Protocol), 165
Unibrain, 29
Uninterruptible Power Supply (UPS),
    49, 80
Universal Plug and Play (UPNP), 196
Universal Serial Bus (USB), 27–29
University of Hawaii (Oahu), 11
UNIX computers, 170–171
Unshielded Twisted Pair (UTP) cables, 32
uplink ports, 48
UPNP (Universal Plug and Play), 196
UPS (Uninterruptible Power Supply),
    49, 80
USB Implementers Forum Inc., 28
USB ports, 27–29
    connecting wireless network cards to, 83
    maximum speed for, 77
    in phoneline networks, 50–51
    as printer ports, 111
USB-to-phoneline adapters, 76
USB (Universal Serial Bus), 27–29
User Datagram Protocol (UDP), 165
user groups, 136–137
users, 137
UTP (Unshielded Twisted Pair) cables, 32

V

video cameras, 199
video compression, 200
video games, 201
video systems, 196, 200

virtual drives, 132–133
virtual network adapters, 29
Virtual Private Networks (VPN), 203
virtual reality, 203–204
viruses, 168–169
voice communications, 196
voice recognition, 207
VPN (Virtual Private Networks), 203

W

water-level sensors, 200
Web browsers, 157, 167
Web pages, 169
Web servers, 155, 168
Web sites
    ActionTec, 28
    Apple Computer, 15
    Cayman Systems, 53
    Digital Marketplace, 107
    EZ-Link, 28
    Furman Sound, 81
    GoDaddy.com, 106
    Iomega, 173
    LG Electronics Inc., 197
    Lockdown, 169
    McAfee, 169
    MSN Messenger, 143
    NTII, 203
    Proxim, 15
    ShareWave, 15
    SimpleDevices, 12
    Symantec, 169
    Unibrain, 29
    Universal Plug and Play, 196
    WildPacket, 85
    Windows XP, 137–140
    Xanboo Inc., 199

Webcams, 21
Webphones, 22
whips, 33
Whirlpool, 197
Whitecap, 15
Wi-Fi (Wireless Fidelity), 14–17, 54–55
WildPacket AiroPeek software, 85
Windows 2000, 113
    Active Directory for, 137
    configuring DHCP servers on, 152–154
    groups in, 136–137
    installing Internet Connection Sharing
        on, 160
    and IP addresses, 96–97
    IPConfig utility, 182–183
    network printing, 115–118
    user profiles in, 134–135
Windows 95/98/ME operating systems
    installing Internet Connection Sharing
        on, 158–160
    and IP addresses, 95–96
    Netstat utility, 184
    network printing, 114–115
    network setup in, 100–102
    print servers, 112
    sharing folders on, 121–122
    WinIPCFG utility, 183–184
Windows Explorer, 166
Windows NT, 96–97
Windows operating systems
    and IP addresses, 95–99
    network setup in, 100–102
    sharing folders on, 121–122
    user profiles in, 134
Windows XP
    Active Directory for, 137
    groups in, 136–137

and IP addresses, 97–99
IPConfig utility, 182–183
network printing, 115–118
print servers, 113
quick switching between users on, 136
Remote Assistant, 141–143
Remote Desktop Connection, 137–141
sharing files on
    Classic File Sharing, 126–128
    Simple File Sharing, 123–126
user profiles in, 135–137
WINIPCFG utility, 149–150, 183–184
WinRoute Pro, 156
WINS proxy, 183
wire trimmers/strippers, 34
wired hubs, 46–47
wired networks, 20
    ethernet, 24–25
    Firewire, 29–30
    home phone lines, 20–23
    planning, 60
    power lines in, 23–24
    USB (Universal Serial Bus), 27–29
    See also home networks; networks;
        wireless networks
wireless DHCP service, 154–155
Wireless Fidelity (Wi-Fi), 14–17, 54–55
wireless infrared ports, 111
wireless Internet, 15
wireless LANs, 53, 85
wireless network cards, 83–84
    setting up, 103–104
wireless networks, 11
    access points, 84–85
    Bluetooth, 18–20
    HomeRF (Home Radio Frequency),
        12–14

installing network cards in, 83–84
IR (infrared), 17–18
planning, 60–62
signal strength in, 85–86
troubleshooting, 190–191
Wi-Fi (Wireless Fidelity), 14–17
See also networks; wired networks; home
    networks
wireless roaming, 155, 202
wireless telephones, 190
word processors, 169
workgroups, 129
World War II, 11
World Wide Web, 165
worms, 169
writeable CD-ROMs, 172–173
writeable DVD-ROMs, 173

X

Xanboo Acoustic Sensor, 200
Xanboo Color Video Camera, 199
Xanboo Door/Window Sensor, 200
Xanboo Inc., 199–200
Xanboo Power On/Off Sensor, 200
Xanboo System Controller, 199–200
Xanboo Temperature Sensor, 200
Xanboo Water Sensor, 200
Xbox, 201
Xbox Gateway, 201
Xerox, 3
Xerox Palo Alto Research Center, 3, 24

Z

Zip disks, 173